CYBERCULTURE COUNTERCONSPIRACY

A STEAMSHOVEL WEB READER

Kenn Thomas, Editor

Volume Two

Cyberculture Counterconspiracy • Vol Two
ISBN 1-58509-126-X

LAYOUT AND DESIGN

Tedd St. Rain

COVER DESIGN

Kevin Belford

"UNTHINKABLE COMPLEXITY"
by Kenn Thomas

"The matrix has its roots in primitive arcade games," said the voice-over, "in early graphics programs and military experimentation with cranial jacks." On the Sony, a two-dimensional space war faded behind a forest of mathematical - ly generated ferns, demonstrating the spa[t]ial possibilities of logarithmic spi - rals; cold blue military footage burned through, lab animals wired into test sys - tems, helmets feeding into fire control circuits of tanks and war planes. "Cyberspace. A consensual hallucination experienced daily by billions of legit - imate operators, in every nation, by children being taught mathematical con - cepts...A graphic representation of data abstracted from the banks of every computer in the human system. Unthinkable complexity. Line of light ranged in the nonspace of the mind, clusters and constellations of data. Like city lights, receding...."

— William Gibson, *Neuromancer* —

    The durability of Gibson's description of the internet testifies to the writer's talent. He wrote it in 1983 and now, in 1999, it's only beginning to seem dated, even though consumer computer technology has evolved through many generations. More advanced military technology still awaits transfer down to the cyberpeonage. *Steamshovel Press* has telegraphed suggestions of it in reports on topics like the PROMIS backdoor variations (1) found on web browsers, and the super-surveillance ECHELON satellite system, portrayed but not named in the movie *Enemy of the State* (2). Gibson's elegant description, of course, has yet to catch up with William S. Burroughs' *Interzone* visions, Burroughs dead since 1997, and cohort Tim Leary, the true champion of the cyberculture, years gone now as well.(3)

    Their presences still beam, however, as *Steamshovel Press* readers jacked into the grid await further surprises from the developing technology. It came as no surprise that the Heaven's Gate webmasters were *Steamshovel* fans. The group's combination of UFO obsession and alienation from the mainstream culture fit the reader profile, albeit in a fatally exaggerated form (4). For the more typical reader, *Steamshovel's* pulp-paper presence began on the newsstands in 1992, although as a small zinelet it's history extends back to 1988. It circulated among the other bygone zines with names like *Ganymedean Slime Mold, Popular Reality, Crash Collusion,* Jim Keith's old *Dharma Combat,* and Greg Bishop's still current *Excluded Middle,* produced by bright minds, anarchists, fanboys, varieties of sex maniacs, religious cultists, and really good graphic artists and writers, already going nuts with the technology of cheap, easy paper reproduction. Those familiar with this history know that this creative frenzy of small publishers blossomed into the *Factsheet Five* phenomenon, and remains quite a contrast to the vapid media

Jim Keith (1949-1999). Longtime *Steamshovel* friend, Jim Keith, fell from a stage during Burning Man '99 and broke his knee. He passed away during surgery at 8:10pm on 07 Sep 99 at the Washoes Medical Hospital in Reno. "Keith himself would certainly have been suspicious of the circumstances of his own death." – Kenn Thomas

dross hardcopy on the magazine stands but rushed also to the new electronic playground. As that activity and energy enlivened the developing electronic technology, *Steamshovel* began to develop its web presence even as it became more of a newstand magazine. The *Steamshovel Press* web site resides at **http://www.umsl.edu/~skthoma**.

The volumes of *Cyberculture Counterconspiracy* collect material posted to the web by *Steamshovel Press* over the past several years. This material has been removed from the web now to make the site less cumbersome, and to make these volumes unique. Appropriately enough, *Cyberculture Counterconspiracy* uses one of the new digital technologies for books, the laser book imprint. These web pages have been submitted to the digital system of a major distributor, where they remain on file until orders come in. *Steamshovel* may print copies one at a time but also can produce thousands of copies for bookstore distribution. At present, this process remains more expensive than regular printing and distribution, but it provides a degree of flexibility unavailable the old fashioned way. *Steamshovel* produces only what it needs to satisfy demand, and the book never goes out of print.

The first volume of *Cyberculture Counterconspiracy* collects the most prominent feature of the *Steamshovel* web site, a column called "The Latest Word." Changed sometimes as frequently as every week, this column includes short informational features, interviews and editorials, by writers like Jim Keith, Len Bracken and Adam Gorightly, and others whose longer pieces often appear in the newsstand *Steamshovel*. It chronicles the Clinton conspiracy era, beginning with the White House report using *Steamshovel* material that led to the coining of the phrase "Vast Right Wing Conspiracy." It includes Peter Dale Scott's definitive analysis of the Lewinsky matter as a military intelligence operation. Some reports, like that on the murder of former White House intern Mary Caitlin Mahoney, include the relevant hyperlinks as inserts on the page. Other insights gathered here involve mind control, Wilhelm Reich, Czechoslovakian spy activity connected to Beat poet Allen Ginsberg, possible alien mathematics secretly coded into the daily *New York Times*, obits for Carlos Castaneda and Kerry Thornley (a long, revelatory interview accompanying the latter), remote viewing and much else.

Volume two contains book, movie and electronic media reviews from the "Offline Illumination" column from the website and "Things Are Gonna Slide", a column, assembling parapolitical news items and theory. Both cover the same period of recent history as the first volume. "Offline Illumination" gives a capsule view of the best literature and electronic media productions of the counterconspiracy culture. It is highlighted by the contributions of Rob Sterling, whose *Konformist* newsletter (**www.konformist.com**) has risen to the top of conspiracy news reporting on the web; and Acharya S who carries on a web discussion about religious conspiracy (**www.truthbeknown.com**). New essays by Sterling, Acharya, Greg Bishop (whose *Excluded Middle* zine now has a web presence at **www.primenet.com/~exclmid/**) and Richard Metzger (his *Infinity Factory* webcast, on the *psuedo* network or via Metzger's **www.disinfo.com** has become a regularly watched program on the desktops of many conspiracy students) are absolutely unique to this second volume--never on the *Steamshovel* web page, never in the hard copy *Steamshovel*. *Steamshovel* takes great pride in having these writers as contributors and web allies. As dharma combatants in the cybersphere, their historical insights are unparalleled.

The all-new section of volume two also highlights the talents of Kevin Belford, an artist whose work has adorned pages of the hardcopy magazine. *Cyberculture Counterconspiracy* includes two of his remarkable graphic presentations, "The Rosetta Solution: The Murder of Officer Tippit" and "The Manson Family Who's Who."

Steamshovel Web readers go to the "Things Are Gonna Slide" column for raw data about the conspiracy culture, as much as possible unfiltered by political, religious or personal agendas. The column's title comes from a Leonard Cohen song, "The Future", which ironically laments the passing of the pre-information age era: "Give me back the Berlin Wall/Give me Stalin and St. Paul/I've seen the future, brother/It is murder/Things Are Gonna Slide/Slide in All Directions/Won't Be Nothin'/Nothin' you can measure anymore..."

Steamshovel shares both the sentiment and the irony of Cohen's intent (5). The info-abyss of cyberspace was imagined early by Harry Truman's scientific adviser, Vannevar Bush, and *Steamshovel* also shares his observation that "Presumably man's spirit should be elevated if he can better review his shady past and analyze more completely and objectively." (6) It offers the two volumes of *Cyberculture Counterconspiracy*, and the continued work on the *Steamshovel* web page, in that spirit.

Kenn Thomas
July 4, 1999

Notes:

1. The story of the PROMIS software, stolen from the Inslaw company and sold illegally by the US to police agencies around the world with a secret built-in capability to spy on those agencies, is told best in *The Octopus: Secret Government and the Death of Danny Casolaro* (Feral House). Casolaro's biography reads like a cyberpunk novel, with protagonist Casolaro lost, and ultimately killed, while delving into the PROMIS cyber environs.

2. Conspiracy topics now proliferate in Hollywood. Oliver Stone used the interest to help create the JFK Assassination Materials Review Board, but by and large this interest has served little social good. *X Files* and Mel Gibson's *Conspiracy Theory* movie continued Steppin' Fetchit-type stereotypes of conspiracy students. Many actors, notably Will Smith, now use the label "conspiracy theorist" as part of their public image. That Smith's movie, *Enemy of the State*, did not contain the word "ECHELON" in any of its script speaks volume. The title of the movie refers to a phrase, "enemies of the state", usually applied to Stalinist ethnic resettlement programs, source of the civil war in the Russian republic of Chechnya. In December 1998, Chechen rebels beheaded three employees of the telecommunications firm Granger Telecom. Rumors circulated widely that the rebels caught the men installing an ECHELON satellite aerial.

Oliver Stone tried to continue his filmic foray into conspiracy with a documentary television program entitled *Oliver Stone's Declassified* for the entertainment division of the ABC network. The program was dropped when Stone insisted on a segment detailing the theory that a missile downed TWA Flight 800 in 1996. *Time* magazine (11/9/98) reported that pressure from "aviation-industry sources" caused ABC's news division to apply enough pressure to have the show cancelled before it aired. Interesting, too, that the subject of Stone's *JFK* movie, Jim Garrison, felt that Kennedy was a victim of the aerospace industry. (See *Maury Island UFO*, IllumiNet Press, 1999.)

3. Perhaps Dr. Leary would have appreciated the irony that the FBI continued its smear against him by releasing on the internet selected documents from

his time in prison, when he provided the Bureau with some information. Leary long acknowledged that he did this, just as he gave due credit to the CIA for helping usher in the psychedelic era. However, it became "news" once again in the Summer of 1999 when a website called *Smoking Gun* posted files documenting that time released to it through the Freedom of Information Act.

Dr. Leary discusses it in his 1983 autobiography, *Flashbacks*, and it's discussed in the Leary/G. Gordon Liddy debate movie, *Return Engagement*. According to Leary, the only people harmed by anything he said were some scumbag lawyers who deserved it. The FBI make an effort to exaggerate this and turn it into a "snitch jacket" for the sake of ruining Leary's future credibility. In fact, while Leary was doing his "informing", several people organized a press conference, PILL (People Investigating Leary's Lies), to denounce it and the situation that had been forced upon him. Allen Ginsberg spoke at this conference. None of the conference organizers were compromised seriously by what Leary said and many remained his friends until his death. Leary knew everyone. If he had "snitched" anything of significance, this would be a much bigger deal than it is.

The allegations had a strange afterlife, however. Walter Bowart, for instance, transformed them into an entirely imaginary scenario of Leary returning to his cell one night after a lobotomy, with blue streaks painted across the temples of his shaved head, now a total mind control slave. This came in a particularly ungracious obituary Bowart wrote for Dr. Tim, Leary's reward for one having given some lurid details about his intelligence community connections for Bowart's book, *Operation Mind Control*.

Another author, Mark Reibling, in a 1994 book called *Wedge: The Secret War Between the FBI and the CIA*, tried to make the case for Leary having been an informant before prison, during his years in exile. I checked Reibling's government document sources and they did not match the details of Leary's biography. Reibling also tried to make the case that Bob Woodward's Deep Throat was actually Cord Meyer, ex-husband of famous Leary gal pal Mary Pinchot Meyer.

The February 1999 issue of *Flatland* recounts my own petition for Leary's FOIPA file. The FBI is still doing its best to make sure that the full file is not released, only "summaries" to a chosen few in the media. The files posted on the web by *Smoking Gun* make every effort, by selection and interpretation, to put the worst possible spin on this episode in Leary's life. For instance, a statement Leary makes about his plans for public life after prison, in most contexts a heroic ambition for him considering the circumstances, has been placed before other testimony about one of those lawyers. This has been done "for clarity"--to make it "clear" that Leary was simply finking for the sake of his own freedom.

4. *Steamshovel* was one of a small number of newspapers and magazines that ran ads paid for by the group containing rants that explained their philosophy.

5. Richard Belzer, whose show business career stretches back to the 1971 *Groove Tube* movie of 70s and forward to his role as Detective John Munch in the TVshow *Homicide: Life in the Streets*, once interviewed Leonard Cohen for his old talk show, *Hot Properties*. He asked Cohen about his favorite band. "Foetus On Your Breath" came the response. Belzer didn't miss a beat with his follow up question about the name of the band's hit song. "My Gums Bleed For You", said Cohen. Belzer's book, *UFOs, JFK and Elvis: Conspiracies You Don't Have To Be Crazy To Believe*, came out in 1999.

6. The essay, "As We May Think," was written at around the time of the Roswell crash and Vannevar Bush's signature can be found on the notorious MJ12 documents. Bush helped frame the developing technology, but his 1947 description of personal computers remains uncanny, especially in its acknowledgement that it is based on projections about the then current technology, as if he has an awareness of an alien technology that he's trying to match to the technology he is familiar with.

Bush says: "Consider a future device for individual use, which is a sort of mechanized private file and library. It needs a name, and to coin one at random, 'memex' will do. A memex is a device in which an individual stores all his books, records, and communications, and which is mechanized so that it may be consulted with exceeding speed and flexibility. It is an enlarged intimate supplement to his memory. It consists of a desk, and while it can presumably be operated from a distance, it is primarily the piece of furniture at which he works. On the top are slanting translucent screens, on which material can be projected for convenient reading. There is a keyboard, and sets of buttons and levers. Otherwise it looks like an ordinary desk.

In one end is the stored material. The matter of bulk is well taken care of by improved microfilm. Only a small part of the interior of the memex is devoted to storage, the rest to mechanism. Yet if the user inserted 5000 pages of material a day it would take him hundreds of years to fill the repository, so he can be profligate and enter material freely.

Most of the memex contents are purchased on microfilm ready for insertion. Books of all sorts, pictures, current periodicals, newspapers, are thus obtained and dropped into place. Business correspondence takes the same path. And there is provision for direct entry. On the top of the memex is a transparent platen. On this are placed longhand notes, photographs, memoranda, all sort of things. When one is in place, the depression of a lever causes it to be photographed onto the next blank space in a section of the memex film, dry photography being employed.

There is, of course, provision for consultation of the record by the usual scheme of indexing. If the user wishes to consult a certain book, he taps its code on the keyboard, and the title page of the book promptly appears before him, projected onto one of his viewing positions. Frequently-used codes are mnemonic, so that he seldom consults his code book; but when he does, a single tap of a key projects it for his use. Moreover, he has supplemental levers. On deflecting one of these levers to the right he runs through the book before him, each page in turn being projected at a speed which just allows a recognizing glance at each. If he deflects it further to the right, he steps through the book 10 pages at a time; still further at 100 pages at a time. Deflection to the left gives him the same control backwards.

A special button transfers him immediately to the first page of the index. Any given book of his library can thus be called up and consulted with far greater facility than if it were taken from a shelf. As he has several projection positions, he can leave one item in position while he calls up another. He can add marginal notes and comments, taking advantage of one possible type of dry photography, and it could even be arranged so that he can do this by a stylus scheme, such as is now employed in the telautograph seen in railroad waiting rooms, just as though he had the physical page before him.

All this is conventional, except for the projection forward of present-day mechanisms and gadgetry."

8

OFFLINE ILLUMINATION

MILABS: Military Mind Control and Alien Abduction (Illumninet Press)

This book opens with a precautionary warning from C.B.Scott Jones that resistance to UFO research may have less to do with actual saucer events than the fact that UFOs may be used to disguise human mind control operations. Dr. Helmet Lammer, a geophysicist and planetary scientist, and Marion Lammer, a law student in Austria, review the familiar MKULTRA and ARTICHOKE projects with a closer look at classified material than many previous attempts. This is especially so in relation to how these notorious psyops continue into the present, via the alien abduction spectacle and with the newer technologies of implants and genetics. The book argues for military over actual aliens, which makes for a scarier thesis. Among its many illustrations, photos, x-rays and other documentation, readers will find a reproduction of the August 17, 1960 memo from MKULTRA Subproject 119, designed "to make a critical review of the literature and scientific development related to the recording, analysis and interpretation of big-electric signals from the human organism" This is the memo that suggests military interest in Wilhelm Reich, one of the first scientists to collect and study such data. The memo was mentioned in the Steamshovel book, Mind Control Oswald and JFK, which reprints the 1968 book on mind control technology called Were We Controlled? MILABS refers also to Were We Controlled? (disappointingly without reference to the value-added Steamshovel version), and otherwise contains reference to the technologies presented there, RHIC and EDOM, based on the work on Jose DelGado. MILABS adds considerably to the mind control library because it brings it into the contemporary framework, including the fascinating research and experience of Melinda Leslie.

LOST CONTINENTS AND THE HOLLOW EARTH

Adventures Unlimited (815) 253-6390. Also available from The Book Tree (800) 700-TREE

Although this book reprints I Remember Lemuria and The Shaver Mystery by Richard Shaver, almost half of Lost Continents and The Hollow Earth consists of original material by the maverick archaeological heretic and historian David Hatcher Childress. Childress spells out the lore regarding UFOs and Antarctica, the tunnel systems in South America and under-the-surface civilization in central Asia. Childress' perpetual circumnavigation of the globe and its mystery spots, as well as his love of rare books and obscure historical sources, make him uniquely valuable in placing the Shaver material in a real world context. He devotes one new chapter to the history of Shaver's volumionus a rant on underground beings called Deros and Teros channeled to a Pennsylvanian welder through his equipment and published in Ray Palmer's pulp magazines of the 1940s and 50s. It offers some biography of Shaver and Palmer, but also looks at the zincs (Shavertron; Hollow Earth Insider) and subculture that evolved around hollow earth speculation, some of it  intensely funny. Steamshovel readers waiting for the release of Maury Island UFO will find this important background reading, as Palmer played a key role in the 1947 events at Maury Island. (An appendix on Shaver written by Conspiracy Nation's Brian Redman will appear in Maury Island UFO.) Another chapter by Childress, "The Search for the Hollow Earth" provides even more expanded historical overview of beliefs and explorations regarding subterranean humanity. The book comes lavishly illustrated—many Shavertron covers and cartoons—and reproduces "I Remember Lemuria" and "The Shaver Mystery" from the pages of the original edition. That alone makes it a good buy. Childress' exercise of his erudition on the the topic, however, makes it—ahem— underground classic.

STEAMSHOVEL PRESS

STRUWWELPETER

Last month SaritaVendetta's exhibition at Los Angeles' La Luz de Jesus Gallery left a profoundly disturbing impression on the gathered art connoiseurs and Feral House party dogs. Vendetta illustrated Struwwelpeter: Fearful Stories and Vile Pictures to Instruct Good Little Folks by Heinrich Hoffman, and published by His Beastliness, Adam Parfrey. Vendetta's visual imagination almost perfectly matches the sadistic qualities of the book.

It reproduces the 1845 children's classic in its entirety from the original book by Heinrich Hoffmann, including a World War II political parody, Struwwelhitler, and introductory exposition by folklore expert Jack Zipes (The Lion and the Unicorn). This edition of Struwwelpeter comes deluxely packaged in 176 thick, glossy, 8x1 1 pages. From the cover copy: "Warning! This Children's Book Is Not For Children! Struwwelpeter [threatens] children with the consequences that befall the disordered and disorderly. Thumbs are sheared off, eyes fall out of sockets, faces are pecked to death and bodies waste to nothing. Though castigated in recent years for its sadistic approach to child-rearing, Struwwelpeter remains a cultural phenomenon . . . translated into many languages, the subject of a popular German museum, and the unmistakable influence of Charlie and the Chocolate Factory, which also disposes of wretched kids in rhyme."

STEAMSHOVEL PRESS

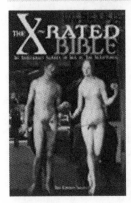

THE X-RATED BIBLE: AN IRREVERENT SURVEY OF SEX IN THE SCRIPTURES
By Ben Akerley Feral House
Reviewed by <u>Acharya</u> S

The X-Rated Bible, a survey of sex in the Holy Bible, is simply one of the best books on the market. It should be mandatory reading, particularly in consideration of the fact that the "Good Book" is pushed worldwide as "God's Word." As "X-Rated's" author, Ben Akerley, points out in detail, the Old Testament is full of sexual perversion, not only on the part of "infidels" but also on that of the "chosen people," whom most people have been led to believe were godly, pious individuals who never did anything remotely "bad." Au contraire! The "great patriarchs" and "heroes" of the Old Testament would be considered perverts and criminals by today's social and moral standards. But the New Testament also does not escape criticism, as Akerley reveals the bizarre and pathological attitudes regarding sex therein as well.

When The X-Rated Bible first came out in 1985, even though it was published by a small company it received some serious attention, and Akerley was forced into debates on radio and TV programs. His critics were unable to point out any serious flaws in his work and research -because he was merely quoting the "Holy Scriptures," not making anything up! For freethinkers and believers alike, Akerley has done a great service, because the Bible is a manual designed to manipulate the masses. The fact that very few believers actually read the "Good Book" and know little about its endless chronicling of perversion and genocide, constitutes proof that it serves as mind-control, as does the fact that those selfsame believers mindlessly believe the Bible is some great, spiritual work because their priests and pastors have selectively fed them "feel-good" passages. In reality, a close examination of the Bible will nauseate all but the most insensate. As the great statesman Thomas Paine said, quoted by Akerley:

"Whenever we read the obscene stories, the voluptuous debaucheries, the cruel and tortuous executions, the unrelenting vindictiveness, with which more than half the Bible is filled, it would be more consistent that we called it the word of a demon than the word of God. It is a history of wickedness, that has served to corrupt and brutalize mankind; and, for my part, I sincerely detest it, as I detest everything that is cruel."

And the eminent freethinker Robert Ingersoll stated:

"Nobody holds with greater contempt than I the writers, publishers, or dealers in obscene literature. One of my objections to the Bible is that it contains hundreds of grossly obscene passages not fit to be read by any decent man; thousands of passages, in my judgment, calculated to corrupt the minds of youth."

Ben Akerley has compiled these various obscene passages in one easy-to-read book that loosens the bonds of erroneous beliefs which have caused inconceivable carnage and turmoil upon this planet. And his wonderful work has now been re-published in a beautifully done layout by the experts at Feral House. The back cover blurb runs, "That's right, friends. We're talking about the Holy Bible, a book filled with incest, rape, adultery, exhibitionism, debauchery, abortion, prostitution, drugs, bestiality, castration, scatology - all the nasty stuff!" In exposing the Bible's "dirty little secrets," Akerley cites scripture, chapter and verse, and explains sexual euphemisms and innuendoes designed to go over the heads of the common folk, which they obviously have. The X-rated Bible is truly a unique book that should be read by all who are interested in what the Bible really says.

THE SECRET BEHIND SECRET SOCIETIES: LIBERATION OF THE PLANET IN THE 21ST CENTURY
by <u>Jon Rappoport</u>
Reviewed by Frank Altomonte

Truth Seeker Company, Inc.; P.O. Box 28550; San Diego, CA 92198, (800) 321-9054. Also Available from The Book Tree (800) 700-TREE

Jon Rappoport, for those unfamiliar with him, is one of those men for all seasons. An investigative reporter by trade, he is really a philosopher at heart. His previous publications, Aids Inc. : The Scandal of the Century, Oklahoma City Bombing: The Suppressed Truth and Madalyn Murray O'Hair: "The Most Hated Woman in America were all investigative in nature, but this latest work is not one of those, entirely. The subject category printed on the back cover is 'Self Actualization'. His more recent book, Lifting the Veil: David Icke Interviewed by Jon Rappoport, is a preview of the format for this latest publication.

In Rappoport's down to earth 'man on the street'style of journalism, we are taken on a journey through one man's time and memory of early experiences that created the foundation for his quest for truth and individual freedom. Along the way we are treated to interviews with people who have belonged to secret societies and those from a different camp, one where the innate power of the individual is manifested and practiced. We are shown how these two camps are in direct opposition to one another, i.e., how the secret societies keep this power from the individual, herding all of society along as common cattle.

The journey begins in Greenwich Village, New York in 1961. Fresh out of Amherst College with a degree in Philosophy, Rappoport was working his last day at a bookstore. In walks a man who asks about books on healing. All they had were books by Wilhelm Reich, if that was what he wanted. The man claimed he had all of those in French and German despite the US ban having been lifted. He makes a remark about Reich being 'on the inside' but having found out a lot for someone in his position. Rappoport a bit of a skeptic points out Reich was a student of Freud who breaks away and dies in jail. The man explains that 'inside' is a relative term but compared to Reich the healing he is referring is '...on Mars. These people don't write books.'This man explains he makes his living by treating sick people. Rappoport, very curious, now has to find out what this man, Richard Jenkins, is talking about. He invites Rappoport to his apartment to watch as he performs on his clients.

For the next year Rappoport is introduced to an unwritten tradition of healing where someone lies down on a table and the practioner, Jenkins in this case, appears to move energy around the person's body using his hands. The people report many things besides a return to health. Some are there simply to explore the effects of this energy manipulation on their minds. Rappoport begins to apprentice. After that year, Jenkins and his wife leave New York to finish their long time search for the origins of this tradition, having told Rappoport of what they had learned so far.

Rappoport continues to treat clients on his own, learning from his own silent inner dialogue when practicing and listening carefully to accounts of their physical and psychic experiences. This 'Tradition of Imagination', as he grew to identify it, becomes the major theme in this book contrasted in depth with its antithesis, the 'Formula of the Secret Society'. We are compelled to join in a search for the beginnings of this tradition. Where did it originate? Who originated it? What else did they know? Rappoport reveals the clues he was given from a personal source, a contact to the forebearer of Richard Jenkins, and looks to the present and reaches back into history and time immemoriam chasing down avenues and corridors for this priceless understanding of a hidden tradition in human history. We visit the Dead Sea Scrolls advanced paranormal powers, Dean Radin, Giordano Bruno and mystical Tibetan Buddhism.

Alongside this theme of the 'Tradition of Imagination'we are also guided through a detailed anatomy lesson on the 'Formula of the Secret Society'. With X-Ray perception, Rappoport spells it out for us. "The tradition is the opposite of the formula of the secret society, a cult, a religion and institution that creates art in order to imprison the mind. The opposite." Being a painter himself, Rappoport attributes the brushstroke of imagination to the powers secret societies wield to create a picture in which everyone of us is framed among the powerful system of archetypal symbols. We are told nothing exists outside the frame and the only way to achieve bliss is through 'us' and our construction of leaders and hierarchies.

We are presented with several eyewitnesses, people who have left cults, a hypnotist and deprogrammer and their stories in first hand interviews of how manipulation according to the formula and its emerging corollaries is effected. Here we get close looks at the Roman Catholic Church, Masonry, The Knights Templar, Theosophy and of course this wouldn't be complete without Nazi Germany and collusion with US investors, CIA and MKULTRA, CFR, Trilateralists and American multinational corporations. That last category is stunning. Rappoport believes and exposes as fact that today our major multinational corporations, e.g. Dow, DuPont, Monsanto, etc., function no differently than secret societies of old.

In the last parts of the book we look at contemporary personalities that personify this 'Tradition of Imagination'. Most memorable was an interview with Ted Clarke, US space program engineer for JPL, who tells us about his fantastic vision for the future. Also text is devoted to hypnotist and deprogrammer, Jack True, who has personally witnessed the affects of the 'Formula of the Secret Society', and further help describe the function and dynamics of this tool. There are in addition several case studies presented of individuals who have chosen to develop their own 'Tradition of Imagination'. The sessions documented by the author are most intriguing, offering the needed motivation for one to experiment on his own.

In summation, this is one man's Opus Magnus. It comes from deep inside, incorporating nearly all of his adult life's work. The book is more than investigative journalism. It is a wake up call; not in the typical sense to become aware of what is going on around you, but a call to wake up to who you really are. It will entertain and at the same time cause you to think and ponder your position in the grand scheme of things as a rational human being, who may have on one occasion considered what this 'rat race' is all about and questioned: 'Is that all there is?'.

MOSES, THEFT FROM EGYPT
By Acharya S

Argh. Here we go again, as millions of children worldwide are programmed with a bunch of hooey, although Dreamwork's "Prince of Egypt" is being presented as an adult cartoon. No matter, as both children and adults will be brainwashed into believing that, unlike the "Lion King," the "Little Mermaid" and other Disney fare, "Prince of Egypt" is a true story about God's "chosen people" and their escape under the marvelous Moses from those evil, nasty Egyptians! Obviously, this is yet more mindless propaganda designed to empower a certain group of people. Yet, the brainwashing is profound, as interviewers breathlessly question producers about how they felt in creating such an epic, which many might consider to border on "blasphemy," and the illustrators themselves giddily admit that this cartoon was more difficult than others "because it really happened."

Horseshit. The Moses story did not "really happen." Like the vast majority of biblical tales, it is a myth based on older tales, changed to revolve around characters of a certain ethnicity or cultural programming, if you will. The Moses tale is, in fact, a plagiarism taken from Egypt and its satellite, Canaan, among others. Moses, then, is not the "Prince of Egypt" but a "Theft from Egypt." Since the ancient Egyptians obviously cannot address this calumny against them for millennia, I will do it for them. The following is an excerpt from my book The Christ Conspiracy: The Greatest Story Ever Sold.

Moses, the Exodus, the Ten Commandments

The legend of Moses, rather than being that of a historical Hebrew character, is found from the Mediterranean to India, with the character having different names and races, depending on the locale: "Manou" is the Indian legislator. "Nemo the lawgiver," who brought down the tablets from the Mountain of God, hails from Babylon. "Mises" is found in Syria, where he was pulled out of a basket floating in a river. Mises also had tablets of stone upon which laws were written and a rod with which he did miracles, including parting waters and leading his army across the sea. In addition, "Manes the lawgiver" took the stage in Egypt, and "Minos" was the Cretan reformer.

Jacolliot traces the original Moses to the Indian Manou: "This name of Manou, or Manes . . . is not a substantive, applying to an individual man; its Sanscrit signification is the man, par excellence, the legislator. It is a title aspired to by all the leaders of men in antiquity."

Like Moses, Krishna was placed by his mother in a reed boat and set adrift in a river to be discovered by another woman. The Akkadian Sargon also was placed in a reed basket and set adrift to save his life. In fact, "The name Moses is Egyptian and comes from mo, the Egyptian word for water, and uses, meaning saved from water, in this case, primordial." Thus, this title Moses could be applied to any of these various heroes saved from the water.

Walker elaborates on the Moses myth:

> "The Moses tale was originally that of an Egyptian hero, Ra-Harakhti, the reborn sun god of Canopus, whose life story was copied by biblical scholars. The same story was told of the sun hero fathered by Apollo on the virgin Creusa; of

Sargon, king of Akkad in 2242 B.C.; and of the mythological twin founders of Rome, among many other baby heroes set adrift in rush baskets. It was a common theme."

Furthermore, Moses's rod is a magical, astrology stick used by a number of other mythical characters. Of Moses's miraculous exploits, Walker also relates:

"Moses's flowering rod, river of blood, and tablets of the law were all symbols of the ancient Goddess. His miracle of drawing water from a rock was first performed by Mother Rhea after she gave birth to Zeus, and by Atalanta with the help of Artemis. His miracle of drying up the waters to travel dry-shod was earlier performed by Isis, or Hathor, on her way to Byblos."

And Higgins states:

"In Bacchus we evidently have Moses. Herodotus says [Bacchus] was an Egyptian . . . The Orphic verses relate that he was preserved from the waters, in a little box or chest, that he was called Misem in commemoration of the event; that he was instructed in all the secrets of the Gods; and that he had a rod, which he changed into a serpent at his pleasure; that he passed through the Red Sea dry-shod, as Hercules subsequently did . . . and that when he went to India, he and his army enjoyed the light of the Sun during the night: moreover, it is said, that he touched with his magic rod the waters of the great rivers Orontes and Hydaspes; upon which those waters flowed back and left him a free passage. It is even said that he arrested the course of the sun and moon. He wrote his laws on two tablets of stone. He was anciently represented with horns or rays on his head."

It has also been demonstrated that the biblical account of the Exodus could not have happened in history. Of this implausible story, Mead says:

". . . Bishop Colenso's . . . mathematical arguments that an army of 600,000 men could not very well have been mobilized in a single night, that three millions of people with their flocks and herds could not very well have drawn water from a single well, and hundreds of other equally ludicrous inaccuracies of a similar nature, were popular points which even the most unlearned could appreciate, and therefore especially roused the ire of apologists and conservatives."

The apologists and conservatives, however, have little choice in the matter, as there is no evidence of the Exodus and wandering in the desert being historical:

"But even scholars who believe they really happened admit that there's no proof whatsoever that the Exodus took place. No record of this monumental event appears in Egyptian chronicles of the time, and Israeli archaeologists combing the Sinai during intense searches from 1967 to 1982 - years when Israel occupied the peninsula - didn't find a single piece of evidence backing the Israelites' supposed 40-year sojourn in the desert.

"The story involves so many miracles - plagues, the parting of the Red Sea, manna from heaven, the giving of the Ten Commandments - that some critics feel the whole story has the flavor of pure myth. A massive exodus that led to the drowning of Pharaoh's army, says Father Anthony Axe, Bible lecturer at Jerusalem's Ecole Biblique, would have reverberated politically and economically through the entire region. And considering that artifacts from as far back as the late Stone Age have turned up in the Sinai, it is perplexing that no evidence of the Israelites' passage has been found. William Dever, a University of Arizona archaeologist, flatly calls Moses a mythical figure. Some scholars even insist the story was a political fabrication, invented to unite the disparate tribes living in Canaan through a falsified heroic past." (Time)

Potter sums up the mythicist argument regarding Moses:

"The reasons for doubting his existence include, among others, (1) the parallels between the Moses stories and older ones like that of Sargon, (2) the absence of any Egyptian account of such a great event as the Pentateuch asserts the Exodus to have been, (3) the attributing to Moses of so many laws that are known to have originated much later, (4) the correlative fact that great codes never suddenly appear full-born but are slowly evolved, (5) the difficulties of fitting the slavery, the Exodus, and the conquest of Canaan into the known chronology of Egypt and Palestine, and (6) the extreme probability that some of the twelve tribes were never in Egypt at all."

The Exodus is indeed not a historical event but constitutes a motif found in other myths. As Pike says, "And when Bacchus and his army had long marched in burning deserts, they were led by a Lamb or Ram into beautiful meadows, and to the Springs that watered the Temple of Jupiter Ammon." And Churchward relates, "Traditions of the Exodus are found in various parts of the world and amongst people of different states of evolution, and these traditions can be explained by the Kamite [Egyptian] rendering only." Indeed, as Massey states, "'Coming out of Egypt' is a Kamite expression for ascending from the lower to the upper heavens."

Churchward further outlines the real meaning of the Exodus:

"The Exodus or 'Coming out of Egypt' first celebrated by the festival of Passover or the transit at the vernal equinox, occurred in the heavens before it was made historical as the migration of the Jews. The 600,000 men who came up out of Egypt as Hebrew warriors in the Book of Exodus are 600,000 inhabitants of Israel in the heavens according to Jewish Kabalah, and the same scenes, events, and personages that appear as mundane in the Pentateuch are celestial in the Book of Enoch." . . .

In addition, the miraculous "parting of the Red Sea" has forever mystified the naive and credulous masses and scholars alike, who have put forth all sorts of tortured speculation to explain it. The parting and destruction of the hosts of Pharaoh at the Red Sea is not recorded by any known historian, which is understandable, since it is, of course, not historical and is found in other cultures, including in Ceylon, out of which the conquering shepherd kings (Pharaohs) were driven across "Adam's Bridge" and drowned. This motif is also found in the Hawaiian and Hottentot versions of the Moses myth, prior to contact with outside cultures. The crossing of the Red Sea is astronomical, expressly stated by Josephus to have occurred at the autumnal equinox, indicating its origin within the mythos.

Moreover, the famed Ten Commandments are simply a repetition of the Babylonian Code of Hammurabi and the Hindu Vedas, among others. As Churchward says:

"The 'Law of Moses' were the old Egyptian Laws . . . ; this the stele or 'Code of Hammurabi' conclusively proves. Moses lived 1,000 years after this stone was engraved."

Walker relates that the "stone tablets of law supposedly given to Moses were copied from the Canaanite god Baal-Berith, 'God of the Covenant.' Their Ten Commandments were similar to the commandments of the Buddhist Decalogue. In the ancient world, laws generally came from a deity on a mountaintop. Zoroaster received the tablets of law from Ahura Mazda on a mountaintop."

Doane sums it up when he says, "Almost all the acts of Moses correspond to those of the Sun-gods." However, the Moses story is also reflective of the stellar cult, once again demonstrating the dual natured "twin" Horus-Set myth and the battle for supremacy between the day and night skies, as well as among the solar, stellar and lunar cults. . . . [end excerpt]

As has been demonstrated, the Moses fable is an ancient mythological motif found in numerous cultures. It therefore has nothing to do with any particular ethnic group, and the character Moses is not the founder of the Jewish ideology. Like so many others, this story as presented represents racist rubbish and cultural bigotry.

Furthermore, rabbis and other authorities have known the mythological nature of this and other major biblical tales, yet they say nothing. Indeed, they go along with it, much to their own benefit. Naturally, the person who discovers this ruse and hoax may rightfully become annoyed, to say the least, at the deliberate deception, and ask "What's up with that?"

Acharya S
Archaeologist, Historian, Linguist, Mythologist Member, American School of Classical Studies at Athens, Greece Associate Director, Institute for Historical Accuracy

STEAMSHOVEL PRESS

THE PHOENIX SOLUTION: SECRETS OF A LOST CIVILISATION BY ALAN E. ALFORD
Reviewed by Acharya S

In The Phoenix Solution: Secrets of a Lost Civilization, author Alan Alford brings novel and interesting insights into the "lost civilization" theory made famous by Plato nearly 2,500 years ago. By his own description a "non-expert," Alford began his quest with a study of the mysteries of the Pyramids and Sphinx of the Giza plateau; soon he was encountering hidden knowledge which revealed, in his words, "that the match between mythology and astronomy is somewhat on the order of 100 per cent." Alford concludes that such knowledge was precise enough to suggest a lost, pre-historic culture of tremendous advancement.

Alford starts his story with the mysterious Sphinx, the date of which has lately been challenged and pushed back thousands of years, ostensibly based on geological observations. This view, of course, is rejected by orthodox Egyptologists, who are not prepared to accept its implications: To wit, that a technologically advanced culture existed eons before the current era of human history. This rejection continues despite the tantalizing evidence presented by such mavericks as von Daniken, John Anthony West, Graham Hancock and Robert Bauval. As Alford points out, it seems unreasonable that the orthodoxy denies the antiquity of Egyptian culture while embracing that of other cultures.

Regarding the Sphinx itself, Alford reiterates the fact that its head is too small for its body and the hypothesis that it had been recarved, possibly millennia after the original, which may have been a lion or, possibly, a dog. As concerns the Great Pyramid, Alford points out that it seems to have been built at the same time as the Sphinx and posits that it is the oldest pyramid in Egypt. The new date of the Great Pyramid thoroughly disturbs the orthodoxy and raises perplexing questions as to construction methods, questions that have always existed, since the Pyramid is among the most astounding feats of engineering ever devised by human hands - how much more astonishing is this feat if pushed back several centuries or millennia?

In his analysis of the age of the Pyramid, Alford dissects and dispenses with the "evidence" of it having been constructed by the 4th Dynasty Pharaoh, Khufu, or Cheops, "discovered" by English traveler Col. Howard Vyse, who claimed to have found "inscriptions" hidden in the "construction chambers" above the so-called King's Chamber. These inscriptions, Alford concludes, are bogus, an opinion concurred with by this reviewer. He also disposes of the cherished notion that all Egyptian pyramids were built as tombs, a belabored opinion that should in all reasonableness be put to rest. Reiterating the words of Bauval, Alford says, ". . . the Great Pyramid has a complexity akin to some giant machine which is beyond our comprehension." To turn the Great Pyramid into a "tomb" built by a megalomaniacal Pharaoh using slave labor degrades it tremendously and buries its magnificent secrets under a mound of the mundane.

Alford hypothesizes that the Great Pyramid, Sphinx and other "ooparts" ("out-of-place-artifacts") were not built by 4th Dynasty kings but were adopted by later dynasties, an idea that causes great distress to Egyptian Egyptologists, who have loathed the idea that anyone but the known Egyptian state built the Great Pyramid, because it implies that another race was involved. It is worthwhile mentioning that the current Egyptian people is not the same as the ancient, so this ethnic pride should not be a factor in any case. Alford asks, "Is it so crazy to suggest that the unique design of the Great Pyramid was a legacy from an earlier, more advanced culture?" He then continues, "In my view, it is certainly less crazy than continuing to believe that the Pyramid was constructed as a tomb for a dead king, and that he built this totally over-engineered and revolutionary wonder of the world with absolute perfection at the first attempt." While marveling at its construction, however, Alford refrains from ascribing this wonder of engineering to "aliens" with superior technology, as is one popular theory of today.

In his examination of the ancient Egyptian religion, although not an expert, Alford does a decent job apparently without the benefit of the important body of work produced by such extraordinary mythicists and experts on Egyptian religion as Gerald Massey, Albert Churchward and Barbara Walker. Alford also displays astute insight as to the duplicity and chicanery of priests, who deliberately change myths in order to establish their superiority over rivals. Whereas so many before him have utterly failed to appreciate the cosmic, rather than mundane and historical, significance of the Egyptian myths, Alford steps up to the plate and gets a hit, although he stumbles and misses the mark on a number of highly important aspects. "Could these 'gods,"' he asks, "represent celestial bodies and their cycles?" - an query to which this reviewer says, "Amen!" If, however, Alford had encountered the works of those great scholars mentioned above, he would not have needed to ask this and other questions, such as whether the enigmatic "Ennead" were the nine planets, because he would have more clearly seen that the ancient Egyptian religion is a version of the ubiquitous, standardized celestial mythos that revolves around the daily, monthly, annual and equinoctial movements of the known heavenly bodies such as the sun, moon, stars and planets, rather than unknown bodies and cosmic cataclysms a la Velikovsky and Sitchin towards whose work Alford fortunately later turns a critical eye. This initial error and oversight undermines Alford's main thesis, however, and makes a significant portion of his book tedious to read, with Alford himself failing to live up to the principle of Occam's Razor ("invent no unnecessary hypotheses").

Alford nevertheless brings some new and valuable insight into Egyptian religion and, by extension, that of many other parts of the world, and assists in restoring the monumental, cosmic signficance of these myths, which have been dismissed and denigrated by later cultures. Also, he does get briefly back on track when he attempts to synthesize the "exploding planet hypothesis" with the important celestial mythos, as well as with his short discussion of freemasonry; for, it is within the secrets of masonry that we will find many of the answers to our questions about ancient and modern cultures. It is masons who built the pyramids and who created the celestial mythos that has been the basis of nearly every religion, as they were also master astrologers, not just astronomers, who encoded their extensive knowledge within the Great Pyramid, which thus serves as a "cosmic computer," as well as a temple of great importance.

This awesome cosmological understanding, then, cries out for the explanation provided by the Lost Civilization Theory. In explaining this lost, technologically advanced culture, Alford suggests that it may have consisted of "wandering nomads" of the type we would expect of space explorers. This nomadic theory would explain why there is little evidence of a "full-blown" civilization at Giza that would allow for an early date for its construction. "Why should we assume that the Sphinx and Pyramids were the brainchild of 'local' sedentary cultures?" he asks, and then continues, "Perhaps we should instead be searching for a wandering race who eschewed the idea of the organised state, being motivated instead by something other than power and vainglory."

In sum, this reviewer enjoyed Alford's book, as it combines scholarship with creative thinking, providing some reasonable solutions to the flaws of both the orthodox and unorthodox opinions concerning these great mysteries of human history. Especially enjoyable is his insistence upon restoring to the ancients their proper level of wisdom and advancement, long subordinated by culturally biased "experts" who have depicted these peoples as little more than cavemen who "accidentally" blundered upon the ability to create amazing and mesmerizing tales and megalithic buildings.

Acharya S is a classically trained archaeologist, historian, mythologist, linguist and expert on the celestial mythos. She is the author of three books, Paradise Found, The Aquarian Manifesto, and The Christ Conspiracy: The Greatest Story Ever Sold. Her website is www.TruthBeKnown.com

www.truthbeknown.com

HAARP: THE ULTIMATE
WEAPON OF THE CONSPIRACY
**Adventures Unlimited (815) 253-6390.
Also available from The Book Tree
(800) 700-TREE**

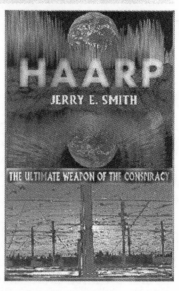

Jerry E. Smith provides the first full-blown conspiracy analysis of the HAARP project since Nick Begich first brought the subject up in his famous book, Angels Don't Play This HAARP. HAARP, of course, stands for High-frequency Active Auroral Research Program, and it consists of an antennae array, still under construction, situated along the Copper River near Wrangell-St. Elias National Park in Alaska. It's just a research facility for topography and upper atmosphere study according to the Department of Defense. Everyone knows better, of course, and the chore has been to figure out its true purpose. Beam weaponry? Planetary defense shield? Mass mind manipulation? Weather control? Tesla technology? Smith asks all of these questions and examines the hard evidence for the plausible ones and the reasons for rumor behind the rest. The book provides a wealth of hard data, with graphics and photos, to help readers understand the reality of the facility but complements that with well- documented speculation about even the strangest possibilities. Smith follows up observations like "[Some] think it will be used by the New World Order to take over the world by projecting holographic images into the sky while beaming thoughts directly into our heads, telling us to accept the 'new' god of their design" with a brief but careful history of the MKULTRA program and mind control technologies like RHIC-EDOM and how they might be applied to HAARP. UFOs enter the discussion, of course, and by book's end Smith examines the roots of UFO Illuminati control in freemasonry and an ancient plot to establish a theocratic world king. Small wonder that author Smith has known Steamshoveler Jim Keith since high school, and even worked in the zine world as part of Keith's old Dharma Combat. HAARP: The Ultimate Weapon of the Conspiracy offers quite a tour de force, but readers need not follow the conspiratorializing to appreciate the science presented as well as the basic facts about HAARP.

STEAMSHOVEL PRESS

FROM OZ TO RAGNAROK
THE LORDS OF CHAOS: THE BLOODY RISE OF THE SATANIC METAL UNDERGROUND MICHAEL MOYNIHAN AND DIDRIK SODERLIND
Review by <u>Robert Sterling</u>

In the novel and film "A Clockwork Orange", a brave New World was predicted, where all of people's material needs are met while true liberty has been destroyed. In response, gangs of nihilistic youths engage in violent and destructive acts, partly because it gives them their sole sense of independence and liberation. By the end of the story, the ruling class has used the youth's ill behavior as propaganda for more restrictions on personal liberty and more control of the people.

In the United States, the urban street gangs have more than lived up to the grim warnings of Burgess and Kubrick, being used as a racial code word and officially sanctioned demon to pass legislation that violates basic constitutional rights. Less has been made here of the mainly (so far) European phenomenon of the Satanic Metal Underground, who fit the Clockwork Orange role so well it should be assumed to be an imitation of sorts. Nearly 100 churches have been torched and desecrated by the head-banging minions of the Black Metal scene, all with barely a word from the korporate media as we head to the end of the millennium. In "The Lords of Chaos", Michael Moynihan and Didrik Soderlind try to shine some light on the black hole of rock music, a light that is long overdue.

As the reviewer is a big fan of the now-discredited musical form known as Heavy Metal - albeit the more pop-flavored brand of the 80's - the book was certainly of interest in seeing where metal has been going since its return to the gutters it came from. Apparently, the reviewer is not alone in his interest: the book has been the hot seller for beastly publisher Feral House since its release, with substantial aid provided by small-penised shock jock Howard Stern (who promoted the tome on his radio show) and his apparently more-literate-than-given-credit-for fans. The appeal is obvious: Satan sells, a fact than Anton LaVey exploted shamelessly until his recent death (an interview with the Church of Satan founder is included in the book.) Add some gasoline and matches, as well as an ugly subculture of a music form that glorifies hedonism and rebellion, and a recipe for a delicious use of paper is the result.

To their credit, Moynihan and Soderlind manage to guide the book through the dark muck wisely. Very easily, this story could be told in a lurid exploitative fashion - "I'm a Metal Satanist and I Burn Down Churches!!!" is a Jerry Springer episode just waiting to happen. (In fact, the book includes articles and pictures from Heavy Metal magazine Kerrang! that revel in such hysteria-mongering.) The other possibility is that the book could have been a dry, scholarly read, reporting the events without catching the flavor of that which is being reported. Avoiding the mistakes of Icarus, the duo present the material in an intelligent and entertaining style that is as fun as it is informative. This reviewer, for one, couldn't put the book down.

Still, reading the book is a frustrating experience. This is not because of the writing, but because of the unfocused anger that the story's protagonist are filled with, anger that fuels their ultimately destructive behavior. It'd be one thing if the Black Metalers were a group of morons. Far from it: Varg Vikernes, the charismatic leader of Burzum and perhaps the central character of this book, clearly is an intelligent guy and has a clue to what's up. So was Euronymous, the late guitarist of Mayhem who was killed by Vikernes, a death that becomes the meat of the book. Even Mayhem's drummer Hellhammer shows himself to be a sharp guy in interviews, no small feat considering most drummers are on par with Tommy Lee in the IQ department. So what the hell is their problem?

A clue is given in the book with the background history behind the sonic attack. Among the more important figures in the evolution tree of Black Metal are blues singer Robert Johnson, as well as Rock gods The Rolling Stones and Led Zeppelin. The key figure, however, appears to be Ozzy Osbourne, the seminal icon of the Metal Milieu due to his ground-breaking band Black Sabbath and his just as impressive latter solo work. Osbourne and Sabbath came out of the hallucinogenic 60's, an LSD-nightmare of gloom and doom that trampled on the flower children's fantasies of peace and harmony with such songs as "Paranoid" and "Iron Man". As their name implies, Ozzy and Sabbath were the shadow of the 60's in full bloom, the dark side that Jagger and Jim Morrison could only hint at in comparison.

Contrary to popular belief (as the book emphasizes) Osbourne and Sabbath were certainly not Nihilist themselves, nor were they Satanists - not even in the LaVey "rational selfishness" sense. His controversial "Suicide Solution" song certainly doesn't glorify killing oneself (though it certainly is sympathetic to those that contemplate it), and "Mr. Crowley" is more condemning than celebratory of the Great Beast himself. The truth is, Ozzy was (and is) a romantic idealist at heart, something which is proven undoubtedly by any examination of his lyrics. It wasn't a rejection of the hippie value system that led to the fury in the Sabbath sound: rather, it was a rejection of the hippie naivete. As Osbourne has since put it, "There was a lot of bullshit going on." Osbourne saw the future too precisely: the military industrial komplex would stamp out any real revolt (Abbie Hoffman, Timothy Leary, The Black Panthers, etc.) and the 60's generation would sell out, become part of the korporate death machine they once supposedly fought against. Foreseeing this bleak future, Oz and Sabbath blared songs that copped an attitude that has since gone multi-platinum.

The problem, of course, is that Osbourne and company weren't trying to glorify nihilism, but to wake people up to what they're really going up against. Maybe something got lost in the translation. Or maybe Vikernes and his ilk, inheriting the future that Oz warned about, are left to senseless violence and destruction as their only option to shock people rather than getting with the program.

The necessity to shock is certainly understandable, but the vehicles the Black Metal adherents use are certainly at fault. Following the lead of Vikernes, the scene is loaded with neo-Nazis, racists, and homophobes, echoing the ugly lyrics whined by Axl Rose in "One in a Million". Bard "Faust" Eithun, a drummer for the band Emperor, is now in prison for murdering a homosexual. His comment: "I have to stand up for what I've done... there's no remorse." Former Mayhem singer "Dead" apparently blew his brains out in a fit of depression. And then there is the Vikernes -Euronymous feud that ended with one dead and the other jailed.

What is revelatory is the participant's discussion of all the deaths and church-burnings, done in a deadpan, nonchalant manner. It's almost as if the Black Metalheads, having embraced a philosophy that life is pointless, have lost any ability to feel emotion about dying or carnage. As Hendrik Mobus puts it after murdering a student, "Every passing second a human dies, so there's no need to make a big fuss of this one kill." This is the real tragedy of this book, that a group of kids who could be among the best and brightest have instead given up caring about anything but shock, perhaps because it is the only thing left that gives them any feeling.

For those looking for conspiracy, it has to be asked if this is by design. After all, in the Burgess novel, it is apparent that Alex and his partners in crimes are unwittingly serving the powers-that-be with their ultraviolence. Likewise, the Crips and Bloods have long been the best poster boys for the prison buildup, higher law-enforcement budgets, and dubious gun-control laws - which perhaps explains the evidence that the weapons and drugs that fuel the gangs come from a higher source, i.e. the CIA. Is someone jerking the Satanic Metal Underground's chain? Perhaps, but the book supplies no such arguments, probably because the evidence is weak or non-existent. Quite the opposite appears true, based on empty boasts of Vikernes on his own importance. Most certainly if there was any deeper conspiracy, he'd be the first to brag about it. An interview with a former OTO leader (an occult organization founded by Aleister Crowley) seems to confirm that the Black Metal isn't run by some larger institution, since these misfits hardly seem particularly well-organized in the first place.

Sad to say the noise of the Black Metal scene - at least its ugliest elements - is pretty pathetic. Faced with a system of evil and hypocrisy, they merely try to one up the system in being diabolical, and fail miserably. These guys aren't stupid, but their anger is totally misdirected. I can't help but think of what a particularly anti-religious friend of mine said when I started describing the book to her: "I want to see churches burned to the ground too, but I want the church members to do it themselves after they realize it's all a fraud." Now there's some real rabble-rousing.

Moynihan and Soderlind deserve at lot of credit for the picture they paint in this investigative work, even if the picture is quite ugly In the end, the Black Metal scene is a sorry-ass attempt by a group of angry young guys to be an individual, and in the process they become all they detest. Sorry, but pentagrams, swastikas, and loud music just don't cut it.

STEAMSHOVEL PRESS

CHUPACABRAS AND OTHER MYSTERIES
by Scott Corrales

Scott Corrales has made several significant contributions to this web site as well as Steamshovel Press magazine. He documented the legend of the Chupacabras, the bizarre Goatsucker beast that haunts Puerto Rico, in various magazines in the Spanish-speaking world, and self-published The Chupacabras Diaries, from which much of the information in this volumes derives. The Chupacabras remains a paranormal phenomenon not well understood where it appears, and even less so with interested US readers. Chupacabras and Other Mysteries provides the first substantive English translation dealing with the bugger. It relies on the research and work of Jorge and Marleem Martin, made first-hand investigations of animal mutilations attributed to the Chupacabras in the Puerto Rican municipalities of Orocovis and Morovis. The book includes a photo section, none of the elusive creatures, but of kittens they "exsanquinated," haunts, and the original sketch based on eyewitness memory. Chupacabras is not a run-of-the-mill hide and seek type Bigfoot. A wide variety of paranormal activity attends its visits. As UFO researcher Marc Davenport points out in the introduction, the creatures' reported eye-beams do not behave in like the bio-luminesence of fireflies and deep sea fish. Chupacrabras is something else again, and this volume contributes greatly to helping figure out what.

INTERRORGATION: THE CIA 'S SECRET MANUAL ON COERCIVE QUESTIONING
With an introduction by Jon Elliston

The Baltimore Sun forced the CIA to release its KUBARK Counterintelligence Interrogation Manual in January 1997 with the threat of a FOIPA lawsuit. The 1963 manual reads like a backdrop to the Costa Gravas film State of Siege and other well-known tales of CIA torture-training, and should also be seen in the context of the CIA memo on "openness" recently surfaced by Greg Bishop's Excluded Middle zinc. The good people at the Parascope web site have reprinted this as a magazine with its text-heavy form alleviated only by the original redactions. It's subject matter is absorbing, however, and revelatory in ways that exceed its look at the brutality of the intelligence world. It's reference to MKULTRA and mind control, for instance, should put it in the footnotes of most future books on the subject. For instance, the bibliography shows plainly that the CIA regarded the "confessions" of downed pilots in Korea as brainwash victims, and studied only the Communist brainwash techniques. No consideration that the pilots were telling the truth about US use of biowarfare. Such blind- sided logic provided the basis for MKULTRA. The bibliography also has reference to John Lilly, famed iso-tanker and ketaminonaut, who left MKULTRAwhen it began exploring electronic brain implants. "After presenting a short summary of a few auto-biographical accounts written about relative isolation at sea (in small boats) or polar regions, the author describes two experiments designed to mask or drastically reduce most sensory stimulation. The effect was to speed up the results of the more usual sort of isolation (for example, solitary confinement). Delusions and hallucinations, preceded by other symptoms, appeared after short periods. The author does not discuss the possible relevance of his findings to interrogation." Fascinating, fascinating stuff, and just the smallest portion of what is available in InTERRORgation.

STEAMSHOVEL PRESS

THE OKLAHOMA CITY BOMBING AND THE POLITICS OF TERROR
by David Hoffman

This enormous compendium of information about the Oklahoma City Bomb contextualizes that event with the data that official investigations and the press have abandoned now that the fix is in and Timothy McVeigh and Terry Nichols have been declared the lone bombers. It supplements Jim Keith's previous work, OKBomb!, in many ways, crissing- crossing what's in that book , adding to its body of knowledge and examining the OKC bomb as part of the "politics of terror" strategy that currently dominates international affairs. It includes an introduction by Oklahoma State Representative Charles Key adapted from an appeal letter that "does not necessarily imply Rep. Key's endorsement of the author's conclusions," noting also that author Hoffman and Key shared investigative leads and information. One conclusion that Key no doubt would affirm is the basic premise of the book: federal agencies know far more about the Oklahoma City bombing than they're willing to admit.

Other than that, readers might quibble about the assessment of guilt relative to right-wing militias or middle east terrorists, but few could argue that Hoffman's conclusions are not based on a wealth of evidence and informed reporting. In fact, Hoffman achieves a level of "triangulation of research" that is quite prescient in the context of the recent embassy bombings in Africa, particularly in light of finger-pointing toward Saudi engineer Osama bin Laden:

"In March of 1995, Israel's Shin Bet (General Security Services, Israel's equivalent to the FBI), arrested approximately 10 Hamas terrorists in Jerusalem, some of whom had recently returned from a trip to Ft. Lauderdale, Florida...interrogation of those suspects was thought to have revealed information concerning the plot to bomb the Murrah Building. The Shin Bet filed a warning with the Legal Attache (FBI) at the American Embassy in Tel Aviv as a matter of course. On April 20, the Israeli newspaper Yediot Arhonot wrote: Yesterday, it was made known that over the last few days, U. S. law enforcement agencies had received intelligence information originating in the Middle east, warning of a large terrorist attack on U.S. soil. No alert was sounded as a result of this information...the BND (German equivalent of the American CIA), also sent a warning to the U.S. State department. That was followed by a warning from the Saudis. A Saudi Major General...informed former CIA Counterterrorism Chief Vince Cannistraro, who in turn informed the FBI. There is a 302 (FBI report) in existence...the Saudi Arabian Intelligence Service reported that Iraq had hired seven Pakistani mercenaries—Afghan) War veterans [like bin Laden, ed.]—to bomb targets in the U.S., one of which was the Alfred P. Murrah Building. They also advised the FBI that—as is often the case—the true identity of the sponsor may not have been revealed to the bombers."

As the "politics of terror" play out on the international stage, readers want to know more than what has been officially proffered, they will need to look at books like The Oklahoma City Bombing and the Politics of Terror.

STEAMSHOVEL PRESS

EVERYTHING IS UNDER CONTROL
By Robert Anton Wilson

Appearances of books by RA Wilson have become fewer and farther between, so a new release seems like nothing less than a major event. The publication of Everything Is Under Control would be a major event anyway, though, since it imparts Wilson's thinking on a long, alphabetical list of conspiracy topics. Best known for his satiric masterwork, the Illuminatus trilogy (co-written with Robert Shea), but also equally celebrated among cognoscenti for many volumes of prosody explicating the future-as-it's-happening (Right Where You Are Sitting Now; Prometheus Rising), this new book summarizes and reviews a large slice of contemporary parapolitical currents. No other writer sees more clearly the fuzzy line between satire and the reality of conspiracy culture. Wilson frames the discussion with a long, insightful introduction linking the uncertainty of the times to the attractiveness of conspiracy theory without dismissing the "theories" or swallowing them whole hog. Wilson's co-author, Miriam Joan Hill, deserves great credit for assembling much of the information from a web site that accepted submissions for several months before publication.

Of course, many facts and theories did not make it in and readers could quibble with some of the discussion about what's in there. For instance, Wilson calls the NASA, Nazis and JFK a "reprint" of the Torbitt Document, when in fact it is the first published edition outside the per order press. In the note about Philip Corso, the retired Army Intelligence office who ostensibly exposed the Roswell military technology project (Tim Leary once said, "I've been working with the technology they gave us since 1963!"), Wilson lists Steamshovel editor Kenn Thomas as a harsh critic. In fact, Thomas was critical of Corso's critics for jumping the gun and not taking full advantage of the colonel's obligation to promote his book, The Day After Roswell. Everything Is Under Control is a not an almanac of conspiracy theories—although it could be used as one—so such criticism is trivial. The book is a think piece that put things into the perspective of Wilson's wit and erudition. He lists "bisociation" under B. for instance, a term that few researchers know. Arthur Koestler coined it for a certain creative process that also happens to inform much conspiracy theory. Steamshovel planned to discuss the idea before being upstaged in this manner, in fact, and may yet examine a few specific examples on the web site soon. So, obviously, Steamshovel readers should tune into Wilson's wavelength.

THE COLLECTED WORKS OF COL. FLETCHER PROULY

With the right hardware and web browser, readers can spend hours exploring the depths of L. Fletcher Prouty's research on and first-hand experience with the JFK assassination and the politics of conspiracy that have followed it for the past thirty years. Prouty served for nearly a decade in the Pentagon and twice that in military service with the Joints Chiefs of Staff, the Secretary of Defense and the U. S. Air Force. Donald Sutherland played Prouty in a much abbreviated version of his relationship with Jim Garrison in Oliver Stone's JFK movie. His work detailing his view of secret government has come under fire because it has been published and reprinted by everything from the Liberty Lobby to the Scientologists. It has never been substantially refuted for its content. At long last an enormous amount of that writing, some of it quote obscured by its publication in alternative sources, has it has been collected here through the laudable efforts of Len Osanic. That includes the complete texts of Col. Prouty's most well-known books, The Secret Team and JFK: Vietnam, the CIA and the Assassination of President Kennedy, with new introductions, a thorough review of the pre-emptive media backlash against Stone's movie, and over six hours of audio and video interviews. Prouty's view of the power elite is shaped by no less a figure than R. Buckminster Fuller, while at the same time his no-nonsense analysis, particularly on POW/MIAs fallout of Vietnam, will appeal even to strident patriot readers.

One example from the CD-ROM's selection of articles:

"[Robert] McNamara and his closest aides were able to take over such key crafts as the iron-bound procurement processes of the military. For more than a year a new fighter plane had been a number #1 requirement of the Air Force. Its primary sponsor was Gen. Frank Everest. At the close of the Eisenhower budget period, carefully executed plans had reserved money in the 1961 budget, for Nixon, that would make more than $3 or $4 billion available for its procurement from the pre-ordained manufacturer, the Boeing Company. Nixon lost, and even after the election of Kennedy and the early arrival of McNamara, it was considered a foregone conclusion that this "Everest" fighter-plane purchase would go through, as planned. We all had much to learn.

It was Nov. 22, 1962, before the McNamara procurement system had run its politically oriented course, with the Secretary of Labor Arthur Goldberg's clever assistance. We learned that the "largest single military procurement program ever" for the TFX or F-111 aircraft, by then a joint Air Force-Navy project based on the concept of "commonality", and for no less than $6.5 billion, had been awarded, by McNamara... not to Boeing, but to General Dynamics-Grumman.

The shock waves in the Pentagon were about the equal of an H-bomb test in the megaton range. McNamara had made his mark, precisely one year before Kennedy died.

To those in the Pentagon, those on Capitol Hill and to others all over the country allied with the Boeing scheme of things, who had planned to help Nixon and his old team spend that $6.5 billion this was an unforgivable blow. One thing those of us in the neutral ranks noted clearly was that the Kennedy "Honeymoon" had ended. "Kennedy" was a dirty word... and this was only 1962."

This same set of circumstances was recently reported by Seymor Hersh as fall-out from blackmail efforts against JFK. (See "Previous Latest Words: JFK on THX.") That's a small sample from an extremely well-done - virtually no technical glitches - and valuable addition to the research library.

STEAMSHOVEL PRESS

ACID: THE SECRET HISTORY OF LSD
By David Black

David Black has contributed a long overdue new history of LSD that does not retread Martin Lee and Bruce Shlain's excellent Acid Dreams (1985) and does not fictionalize the topic like other recent books (Wisdom's Maw). ACID, in fact, is the first piece of substantial research and writing about the figure of Ron Stark, international drug supplier, since Stewart Tendler and David May's obscure book, The Brotherhood of Eternal Love (1984). Stark worked with the Brotherhood, ostensibly overseeing the transformation of acid consumption from recreational pleasure to international mafia marketing and black profiteering. Author Black sets out to track Stark's career and who was behind his emergence as an LSD don during this process. In so doing, he recounts among other things the experiences of Chicago born psychology and parapsychology student Steve Abrams, a major source for much of the information here. Abrams not only corresponded with Carl Jung about synchronicity in the late 1950s, but he was on hand as J. B. Rhine corresponded with Richard Nixon; lectured on ESP in Leningrad at the invitation of the neuroscientist Vailiev, whose work informed Lincoln Lawrence's Were We Controlled?; and started Arthur Koestler off in a direction that ended with Koestler teaming up with Tim Leary for a mushroom experience. Any reader who thinks this history has been mined for all of its pertinent and fascinating detail, concerning MKULTRA, the Human Ecology Fund, and most especially the criminal and entrepreneurial activities of Stark, will be quite surprised by this book. In 1975 Stark was arrested on drug charges in Italy, and this book's chapter illuminates that period with new information on his P2 Masonic Lodge connections and Stark's prediction of the kidnapping and assassination of Italian PM Aldo Moro. ACID adds voluminous information about the "strategy of tension" during this period of Italian history, one so similar to the post-OKC Bomb US political climate, as noted and discussed in Len Bracken's recent work. As history and as sub-text to current affairs, this books makes an extraordinary contribution. It leaves open the possibility that Stark still may be alive. [An additonal note: The book's back cover calls Timothy Leary one of Mary Pinchot Meyer's former lovers, a claim that has not been made previously. Even Leary never suggested that he shared a girlfriend with JFK.]

Available from: VISION Paperbacks a division of Satin Publications Limited20 Queen Anne Street London W1M OAYE-mail: <u>100525.3062@com-puserve.com</u>

steamshovel press

WHITEWASH: A MUSICAL REVUE OF THE JFK ASSASSINATION COVERUP
by Paul Kangas, with Joe Tate,
Mr. X, J. R. Ryan, Rabia, the Bongos

This compilation comes from Paul Kangas, whose essay on George Bush's connection to the JFK assassination was reprinted back in Steamshovel Press #4. He wants to use this music in part to take advantage of George Bush, Jr.'s presidential bid to publicize the information in that essay. Whitewash is an extraordinarily humorous collection of reggaefied tunes that present in song details, ideas, theories and facts about the JFK assassination. Just as a for instance, check out these lyrics from the tape's best track, "Three Little Tramps": "Could the tall one by Jimmy Shlesinger?/And what about the runt?/Could it be a Dicky Helms/Or maybe Howard Hunt?/The one in front, we'll never know/Does he look like Ross Perot?....Lee Bowers was in the railroad tower/In Dallas on that day/He gave eyewitness testimony/About how Jack got blown away/He was overlooking the grassy knoll/Where he saw the riflemen stroll/He took a look and his blood ran cold/This is what Lee Bowers said: "I saw the smoke/I heard the report. There's trouble in the land/An ambush of the president, I just don't understand/After Bowers testified to the Warren Commission/His automobile ended up in a very funny position/It lost its transmission/And he ended up in a funny position/Dead. Very dead. DOA" There's a level of detail here not found in most popular music about the event, delivered in a funny way but with good scholarship and a serious point. Whitewash re-animates the assassination and its lore, demonstrating again its continued rock'n'roll relevance to today's politics, even as Bush himself attempts to recede into history. The revue ends with a lecture rant by Kangas called "Prosecute Bush!" It may seem dated to some, but everyone knows that Bush is still out there affecting things, and the questions that this tape is dedicated to remain important. Bongos founder Rob Norris and his songwriting partner Jeff Cohen contributed "Public Execution" after viewing the Stone JFK movie, saying that it catalyzed their feelings into creating a primal scream of furious anger on the order of the Beatle's "Revolution." The tape can be ordered from Paul Kangas' radio station in San Francisco, KPOO- FM.

STEAMSHOVEL PRESS

THE BIG BOOK OF SCANDAL!
by Jonathan Vankin and 50 Artists

It follows logically that Jonathan Vankin has written a comic book— actually, one of those large paperbacks with 50+ stories, all by different artists, including a few heavyweights like Dick Giordano, Marie Severin, Joe Staton, Paul Gulacy and Walt Simonson. Steamshovel has commented previously on how Vankin's writing style, and that of John Whalen, his partner at Conspire.Com, looks so glibly at conspiracy material it runs a risk of trivializing it all. A 1 37-word wrap up of the Lewinsky week ending 2/15198 by Whalen recently appeared in the New York Times "Sunday" page, where quick hits

on the conspiracy culture actually have become less and less dismissive. That's OK — in measure. Steamshovel readers no doubt laugh until they cry over some of the content of the magazine, and will also at some of what's in this book. It takes a sense of humor as well as a fine-tuned sensitivity to the tragic to deal with vile conspiracy politics. Moreover, putting it all together with pictures and word balloons can make conspiracies digestible to readers unable to handle straight text. In fact, The Big Book of Scandal! contains more credible research than many textual sources.

Vankin does a great job of concisely and completely dealing with long forgotten scandals, without too much crossover into his previous books (Conspiracies, Cover Ups and Crimes and 60 Greatest Conspiracies) and he does not pick easy targets. The Lockheed Scandal, the Wilson-Terpil Affair, several minor celebrity sin-fests, even something on tired old Watergate get comicized here. The book focusses on Hollywood, society, political and big business scandals, and so distiquishes itself from the Big Books on the unexplained, criminals, martyrs, urban legends, weirdos, losers and freaks. (To coin a Vankinish observation, that list looks more like readers than topics the longer it gets.) The first book in this series—from Factoid Books, a front for Paradox Press, which is an imprint of DC Comics—The Big Book of Conspiracies, contained many references to Steamshovel Press, and Steamshovel later outed writer Doug Moench as an early member of the Merry Marvel Marching secret Society.

STEAMSHOVEL PRESS

MIND CONTROL, WORLD CONTROL AND BLACK HELICOPTERS
by Jim Keith

Jim Keith, erstwhile Dharma Combatant whose book output since the baby days of his old zine has been monumental, checks in with two views of the ' Con as varied in style as they are in content. In Mind Control, World Control, I Keith gives a panoramic history of mind control technology as developed and applied by power elites in various attempts to dominate the world. In Black Helicopters II: The End Game Strategy Keith refines a vision about the point and purpose of the mysterious whirlybirds that he set forth in a previous volume.

Mind Control, World Control presents an almost breathtaking vista of historical data interweaving conspiracy lore with familiar history, about electronic implants, behaviorism, psychedelic drugs, making insightful new connections. The book starts with a review of the writings of H. G. Wells, whose science fiction has eclipsed in history other pre-occupation—reflected in such titles as The Open Conspiracy and New World Order. It moves through the establishment of Yale's Skull and Bones (and it's origins in Weishaupt's Illuminati), to the funding of eugenics experiments by the Rockefellers, on to the OSS, Dulles the CIA, Tavistock and into contemporary brainwashing ops, such as Operation Monarch, and even possible mind control applications of the HAARP array.

In order to put this arsenal of information at odds with the global conspiracy state, Keith transforms Wells and other literary stalwarts such as Aldous Huxley from reporters upon trends in mind control technology in their time to propagandists for it. The book reaches its low point when it repeats Walter Bowart's utterly unsupported

Jim Keith (1949-1999)

charges against Timothy Leary in this regard, although at the same time it brings up Billy Mellon Hitchcock, whose familial ties to Richard Mellon Scaife give the book an unforeseen connection to the current conspiracy strife in DC. In fact, the sections in Mind Control, World Control that deal with the history of psychedelic drugs carry an anti-drug message worthy of a federal program, Keith no doubt pandering to a segment of his audience.

Of Black Helicopters II, a Steamshovel reader who works as a software engineer for Boeing says it looks like a compendium of newsletters and briefing documents he and his co-workers receive regularly on the job. That's a testament to the amount of technical information about known and identifiable military hardware in the book.

Keith frames it with further questions and speculation about the unknown aspects of the black choppers, some re-hashed like the connection to cattle mutes and UFOs, but others, like the Quadrant Sign Code and the Endgame Strategy that inject new energy into the debate. The books ends with a call for non-violent resistance to New World Order oppression as perceived and expressed in the black helicopter imagery.

STEAMSHOVEL PRESS

FLATLAND!

Flatland magazine suffered from the same financial body-blow delivered to the entire zine world when the Fine Print distributors went bankrupt late last year, a blow that still has Steamshovel Press reeling. Flatland 15 is the comeback issue, dedicated by editor Jim Martin, in fact, as "the Fine Print" It reflects some of the lingering effects of the Fine Print debacle: the cover is not slick and not in color. According to the editorial, Flatland no longer gets distributed to newstands, but a last-minute deal with the Desert distributors kept this issue on the stands.

It's late in coming—which after all is always true of a zine of such consistently high quality content. Nothing on Monica Lewinsky gets in the way of Flatland 15's 60+ packed pages of repressed and secret evidence review. Martin interviews Peter Robbins,co-author with Larry Warren of last year's most interesting UFO book, Left At East Gate. That book told the story of the Bentwaters UFO incident as experienced by Warren, an Air Force security police officer at the Bentwaters base. Robbins, who has done much level-headed research into UFOs, as well as Wilhelm Reich, gave voice to Warren's narrative. It not only details the incident, including connection to Reichian cloudbusters, but tells of how it affected Warren's life and career afterward. Among other things, Warren was a friend of the late blues guitarist Stevie Ray Vaughn, who shared his interest in UFOs.

Flatland 15 also contains an interview—supplemented by a "Fantasy Analysis of the Nixon tapes"—with psychohistorian Lloyd deMausse, who argues that people remember where they were when JFK died because "we don't want people to think we did it!" Kenn Thomas contributes an up-close examination of the Great Salad Oil Swindle, and Ed Gehrman reports upon biowarfare experimenters with out-of-control moral compasses. A mysterious "Dr. X" contributes an article exposing RDF, "rapid death factor", and some of the horrible reality behind the processing and marketing of blue green algae harvested in Klamath Falls, OR.

Ain't no Fine Print fuck up gonna keep fiesty Flatland from telling it like it is!

Flatland #15 is available from Flatland, POB 2420, Fort Bragg, CA95437. Check out the Flatland Books website at <u>flatlandbooks.com.</u>

Things Are Gonna Slide!

PROUTY HYPOTHESIS DISCUSSED

The following appears in "Edward Lansdale and the American Attempt To Remake Southeast Asia, 1945-1965", a dissertation by Jonathan Nashel submitted the State University of New Jersey in May 1994: "To my eyes, at least, the man at the far right [of the 'tramps being escorted' photo] could be Lansdale, but even if it can be established that this photo 'captures'Lansdale, what does it prove other than that he was on the Grassy Knoll moments after President Kennedy was killed? Champions of Lansdale could easily counter that he was trying to thwart the assassination and arrived too late to prevent the tragedy."

The above photo also appears in the dissertation, although reproduced here from *Edward G. Lansdale A Catalog of His Books and a Register of His Papers at the Air University Library,* Compiled by Robert B. Lane and Delores R. Bynum, Maxwell Air Force Base, January 1989

Ed Lansdale; Andy Messing, Jr., executive director, National Defense Council; Medardo Justiano; Major General John Singlaub; Lt. Col. Oliver North.

The Lansdale catalog reflects that Lansdale owned inscribed copies of *Human Nature and Political Systems* (1961) by Hadley Cantril, the MKULTRA scientist whose work is discussed in the *Steamshovel* book, *Flying Saucers Over Los Angeles*; and *The Hotel Tacloban* (1984) by Douglas Valentine, whose book *The Phoenix Program* appears in the footnotes to the *Steamshovel* book, *The Octopus*.

CLINTON AIDS-TAINTED BLOOD TRAIL II
By Mark Kennedy, The Ottawa Citizen
Sunday 4 October 1998

More thanks to Brian Redman of <u>Conspiracy Nation</u> for this follow-up to the Clinton AIDS story being developed by the *Ottawa Citizen*.

Clinton pal tied to blood scandal.

Vince Foster suicide linked to Arkansas tainted plasma sales.

The controversy over how a U.S. firm collected tainted blood from Arkansas prison inmates and shipped it to

Canada has spread to Vince Foster — U.S. President Bill Clinton's personal confidant who committed suicide in 1993.

Mr. Foster, a boyhood friend of Mr. Clinton's, was one of the president's most trusted advisers. As a corporate lawyer in Arkansas, he worked in the same law office as Hillary Rodham Clinton and became a close colleague of hers.

When Mr. Clinton left Arkansas for the White House in early 1993, he called on Mr. Foster — known as an earnest individual with high ethical standards — to join him as deputy White House counsel. Mr. Foster obliged, also remaining the Clintons' personal lawyer. Now, five years after his mysterious death, two developments have prompted questions about Mr. Foster's knowledge of the U.S. company's prison-blood collection scheme:

- There are signs that Mr. Foster tried to protect the company called Health Management Associates (HMA) more than a decade ago in a lawsuit.

- And a major U.S. daily newspaper recently reported that Mr. Foster may have been worried about the tainted-blood scandal, which was just emerging as a contentious issue in Canada, when he killed himself in July 1993.

Mr. Clinton was governor of Arkansas when the Canadian blood supply was contaminated in the early and mid-1980s. He was familiar with the operations of the now-defunct HMA, the Arkansas firm given a contract by Mr. Clinton's state administration to provide medical care to prisoners. In the process, HMA was also permitted by the state to collect prisoners' blood and sell it elsewhere.

HMA's president in the mid-1980s, Leonard Dunn, was a friend of Mr. Clinton's and a political ally. Later, Mr. Dunn was a Clinton appointee to the Arkansas Industrial Development Commission and he was among the senior members of Mr. Clinton's 1990 gubernatorial re-election team.

The contaminated prisoners' plasma — used to create special blood products for hemophiliacs — is believed to have been infected with HIV, the virus that causes AIDS. As well, it's likely the plasma was contaminated with hepatitis C.

Any information linking Mr. Foster to HMA and its blood program is bound to raise more questions about how much Mr. Clinton knew.

Michael Galster, a medical practitioner who did contract work for the prison system, has revealed to the Citizen that Mr. Foster once approached him in the mid 1980s to ask for a favour.

At the time, Mr. Clinton's administration and HMA were facing a $12-million lawsuit from a prisoner whose infected leg had been amputated at the hip in 1982.

The inmate was claiming that poor medical care by an HMA doctor — who had been working in the prison despite being denied a permanent licence to practice by the state medical board — had resulted in the needless amputation.

Mr. Galster, an expert in prosthetics, says HMA's medical director had asked him to build a special artificial leg for the prisoner in the hope that it would lead to an out-of-court settlement. Mr. Galster refused to get involved, and was visited several weeks later at his office by Mr. Foster, who appealed again for his assistance.

"The purpose of his being there was to convince me to take this, smooth it over and everybody would be happy," says Mr. Galster, who has written a fictionalized account of the prison-blood collection saga, called Blood Trail.

"I refused him. He said, 'I understand your predicament, but this could make it difficult for you to get a future state contract.'

"If it's like the past state contracts I've had, I don't need any," Mr. Galster says he replied. "He (Foster) kind of laughed and said 'OK, I appreciate your time.' "

It was the only time the two met, but Mr. Galster now says he believes Mr. Foster was trying to protect both Mr. Clinton and HMA from public embarrassment.

The questions surrounding Mr. Foster became even more intriguing when, several days ago, the New York Post published an article entitled "The tainted blood mystery" by one of its columnists, Maggie Gallagher. She reported on how the Citizen had broken a lengthy story in mid-September about the Arkansas prison-blood scheme.

Most significantly, Ms. Gallagher wrote that the story suddenly cast new meaning upon "a strange little memory fragment" that had been "meaningless in itself."

Citing a source who asked not to be identified, Ms. Gallagher reported that a day or two after Mr. Foster died on July 20, 1993, someone called a little-known phone number at the White House counsel's office where Mr. Foster had worked.

"The man said he had some information that might be important," wrote Ms. Gallagher. "Something had upset Vince Foster greatly just days before he died. Something about 'tainted blood' that both Vince Foster and President Clinton knew about, this man said."

Mr. Foster's mysterious death spawned a political controversy from the moment that police, responding to an anonymous 911 caller, found his body in a national park in Washington, D.C.

Police concluded that Mr. Foster had stood there coatless in the late-afternoon heat, inserted the muzzle of an antique Colt 38. revolver into his mouth and pulled the trigger. Immediately, conspiracy theorists began spreading rumours that Mr. Foster had been murdered. But independent counsel Robert Fiske (a special prosecutor who examined the Whitewater scandal before being replaced by Kenneth Starr) conducted his own review and agreed with police that it was suicide.

It was believed that Mr. Foster had been suffering from depression and was especially perturbed by a brewing scandal in which he was embroiled. In the so-called Travelgate fiasco, Clinton aides had fired several veteran White House travel-office employees as part of an alleged attempt to give the lucrative travel business to Arkansas cronies.

However, Ms. Gallagher's column has raised questions over whether Mr. Foster was distressed about something he knew regarding tainted blood, and whether this anxiety contributed to his suicide.

In Canada, the summer of 1993 was a critical period. A Commons committee, which had conducted a brief review of the tainted blood scandal, had just released its report in May. Its first recommendation called for a major "public inquiry" to conduct a "full examination of the events of the 1980s" when the Canadian blood supply became contaminated with AIDS.

Indeed, on Sept. 16 — eight weeks after Foster's death — the federal government announced the public inquiry, to be headed by Justice Horace Krever. During the course of his work, Justice Krever unearthed the Arkansas prison-blood collection scheme and wrote about it in his final report last year.

However, no mention was made of Mr. Clinton until last month's story in the Citizen, which drew on documents obtained from Arkansas State Police files.

Copyright 1998 The Ottawa Citizen

STEAMSHOVEL PRESS

LOCH NESS MINISUB
EXPEDITION PICKS A PASSENGER
Loren Coleman Heads For
Loch Ness 03 October 1998

PORTLAND, Maine: The pursuit of one of this century's most enduring mysteries, the Loch Ness Monster, may be closer to being solved. Dan Scott Taylor, Jr.'s minisub expedition has picked internationally known cryptozoologist Loren Coleman to come along for the ride. Taylor, who built the original "yellow submarine" to seek Nessie in the 1969 expedition sponsored by World Book Encyclopedia, is building a bigger minisubmarine to "finish the job we set out to do in '69," notes Taylor. And he has invited Coleman along as a technical observer.

The Nessa, as the submarine will be christened, takes its name from the Gaelic Goddess of Water, Nessa, after whom the River Ness, Loch Ness, and the Monster, Nessie, were named. The Nessa Expedition plans to launch the minisub in June 1999. Nessie sightings go back at least to 565 A.D., and continue to this day. The Nessa Expedition will attempt to return with film, sonar and tissue sample proof of the creatures' existence.

In 1969, Dan Taylor operated his self-built, one-man sub, the Viperfish, in the murky waters of Loch Ness. Taylor soon discovered, despite hints of a couple intriguing encounters, that this earlier sub was too small, too slow and lacked the battery capacity to complete the mission. Taylor hopes to have more success with the Nessa, a larger, more mobile, swifter underwater craft. Taylor has sold his house, already sunk a quarter of a million dollars into the new adventure, and has been very busy working on completing the minisub's construction. His compelling story has been a focus of increasing media interest.

Taylor who was recently interviewed by NBC Dateline came away intrigued when the program did a national survey of marine biologists and cryptozoologists, and picked the passionate, scholarly professor Loren Coleman, a four decades veteran of cryptozoology research and pursuits, to be interviewed. Taylor talked to Coleman after the filming, and Taylor invited Coleman on board the sub in his quest of the Nessie animals.

As it turns out, Taylor discovered, Loren Coleman is a filmmaker, as well as an honorary member of several cryptozoological organizations, and a Life Member of the International Society of Cryptozoology. Coleman has been on several investigations for undiscovered species since the yeti and loch monsters caught his interest in 1960, leading him to travel throughout the United States, Canada, Mexico, and the Virgin Islands interviewing witnesses and gathering evidence of lake monsters, Sasquatch, black panthers, and other creatures.

Coleman contributes a regular cryptozoology column, "On the Trail," to a London-based magazine. He has written seven books on these mysteries, including a biography of Texan millionaire Tom Slick who searched at Loch Ness in 1937, a new field guide to Bigfoot due from Avon next Spring, and a cryptozoology handbook being published by Simon and Schuster during the summer of 1999.

Coleman says: "This is a once-in-a-lifetime opportunity to search for the Loch Ness Monsters. It truly is something that every scientific cryptozoologist dreams about, and I'm overjoyed with Dan Taylor's invitation.

For further info, contact: Loren Coleman phone: 207-772-0245 email: LCOLEMAN1@maine.rr.com

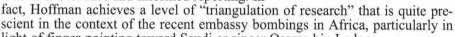

US STRIKES BIN LADEN

Before the recent US bombings in Sudan and Afghanistan, *Steamshovel* posted the following in a review of David Hoffman's book *The Oklahoma City Bombing and the Politics of Terror:*

Readers might quibble about the assessment of guilt relative to right-wing militias or middle east terrorists, but few could argue that Hoffman's conclusions are not based on a wealth of evidence and informed reporting. In fact, Hoffman achieves a level of "triangulation of research" that is quite prescient in the context of the recent embassy bombings in Africa, particularly in light of finger-pointing toward Saudi engineer Osama bin Laden:

"In March of 1995, Israel's Shin Bet (General Security Services, Israel's equivalent to the FBI), arrested approximately 10 Hamas terrorists in Jerusalem, some of whom had recently returned from a trip to Ft. Lauderdale, Florida...interrogation of those suspects was thought to have revealed information concrning the plot to bomb the Murrah Building. The Shin Bet filed a warning with the Legal Attache (FBI) at the American Embassy in Tel Aviv as a matter of course. On April 20, the Israeli newspaper Yediot Arhonot wrote:

Yesterday, it was made known that over the last few days, U. S. law enforcement agencies had received intelligence information originating in the Middle east, warning of a large terrorist attack on U.S. soil. No alert was sounded as a result of this information...the BND (German equivalent of the American CIA), also sent a warning to the U.S. State department. That was followed by a warning from the Saudis. A Saudi Major General...informed former CIA Counterterrorism Chief Vance Cannistraro, who in turn informed the FBI. There is a 302 (FBI report) in existence...the Saudi Arabian Intelligence Service reported that Iraq had hired seven Pakistani mercenaries—Afghani War veterans [like bin Laden, ed.]—to bomb targets in the U.S., one of which was the Alfred P. Murrah Building. They also advised the FBI that—as is often the case—the true identity of the sponsor may not have been revealed to the bombers."

CASOLARO'S GHOST I
OCTO-OSAMA

Note that media have been describing Osama Ben Laden as an example of a new kind of transnational terrorist, "beholden to no nation or ideology, self-financed and savvy about weapons, tactics and technology." It sounds a bit like Casolaro's Octopus.

Osama Ben Laden has his sights set on the Saudis, of course, which provides another—albeit remote-thread to the Octopus research., via the Al Yamama contract umbrella. The Al Yamama contracts sustain the

Saudi royal family in its corrupt wealth and keep the British aerospace industry in business. It's difficult to understand, but the Saudis buy substandard military hardware (planes, etc.) with loans from Britain itself that cover far more than the cost. The threat that Mohamed El Fayad posed to this arrangement was probably the reason behind the hit that killed his son and Princess Diana. One suspected architect of that possible assassination is El Fayad's brother-in-law, Adnan Khashoggi. Khashoggi spent much of his career developing the Al Yamama contracts, and Danny Casolaro was investigating him on the day he [Casolaro] was found dead.

Another more obscure aspect of this unifying conspiracy theory concerns biowarfare. A childhood friend of Khashoggi's headed one of the expeditions to the North Pole to recover RNA residue from the frozen corpses of the victims of the 1918 Spanish flu epidemic. Another such expedition was mounted by the US Armed Forces Institute of Pathology. *New Yorker* covered this story last fall but for some reason it has emerged again in recent news reports.

Richard Sauder discovered that Ron Brown owned the patent for an AIDS-like retrovirus. One of those who died in the Kenya embassy bombing was a virus specialist from the Centers for Disease Control in Atlanta, and another mysterious "administrative assistant" had previously almost died in a crash of a flight that she decided not to take at the last minute. A similar pattern happened to Mohammed Ferrat, an Algerian business associate of Ron Brown (note that Osama ben Laden also has many Algerian business contacts), who was scheduled but to travel on the flight that killed Brown but failed to show at the last minute. Ferrat later died on Flight 800. During the investigation of that disaster, the FBI gave Ferrat special attention, ostensibly because only his last name was listed on the passenger manifest.

In April, Kathleen Janoski, former chief forensic photographer for the Armed Forces Institute of Pathology, provided the Bob Grant Show (WOR, New York) eerie details in the following description of AFIP's handling of reports from investigators in Croatia about the condition of Ron Brown's body:

CALLER: And then Lt. Cogswell was dispatched to Croatia the next day, right?

JANOSKI: Well actually, Lt. Cogswell saw Brown's body briefly that Sunday. He left Dover Sunday and drove back to the Washington, DC area. They flew out of Washington Sunday night and they arrived in Germany on Monday.

CALLER: The point of my question was, at some point Cogswell called back to Dover and told (Col. William) Gormley (the ranking AFIP doctor at Dover) that he couldn't find anything at the crash site that would explain that headwound and told him that Brown should be autopsied. By that point, was Ron Brown's body still even at Dover? Could it still have been autopsied or had they already shipped the body out?

JANOSKI: The body had already been embalmed and it had been released to the funeral home. So at the time that conversation took place, Ron Brown's body was no longer at Dover.

CALLER: So Gormley never even intended to rely on what Dr. Cogswell had to tell him, did he?

JANOSKI: No, not at all. As a matter of fact Cogswell said he couldn't find any- thing to match the wound at the crash site. Everything was either too big or too small to have caused the headwound.

STEAMSHOVEL PRESS

CASOLARO'S GHOST 2
Wackenhut Invades England

Steamshovel encourages readers to review Casolaro's interest in Wackenhut, the security firm that protects Area 51 and its involvement with the Cabazon/Wackenhut joint venture that involved the PROMIS software and led to the deaths of Cabazon tribal leaders.

From *Private Eye*, 21 August 98:

Home secretary Jack Straw is getting into bed with some rum types while building private prisons - people like the Florida-based Wackenhut Corporation. Straw has just announced that Wackenhut is preferred bidder to build and run one of his "secure training centres" for 12 to 14-year-olds in Medomsley, Co Durham. Wackenhut is also preferred bidder for a £32m y oung offenders' institute at Pucklehurst, near Bristol. It already operates at Lowndham Grange Prison and has been managing Doncaster jail since 1995. However, Wackenhut has had links with far right organisations and a history of practices that appear diametrically opposed to the few principles left to "new" Labour. It once made money from holding files on 2.5 million Americans which employers could check to ensure they had no "subversives" on their payroll. And when blacklisting was investigated in the 70s, Wackenhut donated its files to the Church League, a far-sight group which continued to check names.

Today Wackenhut's National Research Centre of Athens, Ohio, offers "pre-employment screening services". And when Aleyska, an oil consortium led by Exxon, was worried by the activities of an environmentalist, Charles Hamel, it hired Wackenhut. The company's agents followed Hamel but their intensive pursuit ended in a law suit. This led to a senate committee concluding that "Wackenhut agents engaged in a pattern of deceitful, grossly offensive and potentially, if not blatantly illegal conduct". Mr Straw's preferred bidder continues to offer extraordinary services in the US. Its "skilled investigators blend in with other workers to become management's eyes and ears in the workforce" and offer the latest "surveillance" devices.

However, Straw may still not save any money. In Texas, where prison privatisation is well-advanced, the department of criminal justice became so tired of being called out by private jails to chase escapers and quell riots it began charging for services. In 1997 Wackenhut paid $10,872 for guards, horses and tracking dogs to hunt an escaper.

Thanks to Mark Pilkington for the above.

CASOLARO'S GHOST III

In light of Casolaro's strong research interest in the human genome project, a DNA database, note the coincidence that the following story has also recently emerged in the UK.

UK News Electronic Telegraph Wednesday 6 May 1998, Issue 1076 DNA database of population by John Steele, Crime Correspondent A national database of DNA samples taken from the entire population was proposed yesterday by a leading police officer. The suggestion by Chief Supt. Peter Gammon, president of the influential Police Superintendents' Association of England and Wales, met with a cool response from Home Office officials and resistance from civil liberties groups. But Jack Straw, the Home Secretary, is prepared to meet Mr Gammon to discuss the issue, and the officer will press his case in a meeting tonight with Alun Michael, the Home Office minister.

Mr Gammon said last night that he recogonised the implications in terms of cost and fears for civil liberties, but he wanted to start a reasoned debate about the proposal. He said: "You have serial killers on the loose, serial rapists. If you can identify them at their first offence, we can save people's lives." Liz Parratt, campaigns manager for the human rights group, Liberty, said: "This proposal represents part of a drift towards policing by coercion."

4 January 1998: DNA tests for business men at risk of overseas kidnap 19 February 1997 - Electronic tagging urged for parents of unruly children 9 February 1997.- Howard to revive ID cards as vote-winner Thanks to Clay Douglas for the above. To find out more about Casolaro's work, read The Octopus: Secret Government and the Death of Danny Casolaro, published by Feral House.

steamshovel press

IS THIS FOR REAL?

Commenting on the the picture to the right, a respected researcher notes that Monica Lewinsky is dressed in hat and coat while most in the crowd have on t-shirts and shorts. Many in the crowd are looking in wildly irrelevant directions (much more noticeable in other photos of this scene.) The figures in the foreground seem

super- imposed. Could this be a *Forest Gump*-styled fake? How much of the Lewinsky scandal, or any public distraction, is created by media manipulators at extremely high tech work stations that put the wonders of home photoshop software to shame? It also calls into question the photograph to the left of Clinton meeting President Kennedy.

STEAMSHOVEL PRESS

APROPOS FROM THE DAYS O'NIXON

From *St. Louis Today*, September 19-20, 1973: Even if President Nixon is forced to release the Watergate tapes, their contents may be worthless as evidence, the Southern California Chapter of the American Civil Liberties Union believes. Citing studies that show how easy it is to alter tapes and how difficult it is to detect such editing, the group argues that the tapes should be destroyed.

New evidence to support pport the contention that tapes can be altered without detection comes from the Canadian Broadcasting

Company, which prepared a special 30-minute tape containing interviews and a musical melody — and then deleted, rearrranged and reconstructed the contents. Examination by 18 experts in North America and England proved that most changes, particularly deletions, were undetectable. The experts concluded that "at the present time, deception techniques are superior to detection rechniques."

The Canadian study is being used in another case where tape recordings have been introduced as evidence. In New Orleans, where District Attorney Jim Garrison is on trial on charges of bribery, Garrison's attorney, F. Lee Bailey, has challenged the admissibility of taped evidence on the grounds that tapes can be altered without detection.

Garrison, who came to national prominence by challengeing the conclusions of the Warren Commission's investigation into the assassination of President John F. Kennedy, contends that he is being framed and that high government officials are "out to get me."

SUBSCRIBE TO *EXCLUDED MIDDLE*

It's Greg Bishop's premiere zine on the scene. The current issue has a long interview with *Steamshovel*er Kenn Thomas; reproduces a fascinating new CIA memo on "Greater Openness" at the agency; interviews Dean Radin, author of *The Conscious Universe*; Scott Corrales on Flying Saucers and Airliners; and analysis by the likes of Paul Rydeen, Adam Gorightly (on Castaneda); Peter Stenshoel; Donna Kossy and others. Write to POB 481077, Los Angeles, CA 90048 or exclmid@primenet.com for order details.

THE VATICAN'S
"MOMENT OF MADNESS"

"Don't shoot this pope! I have to spy on him for the Stasi!" Alois Esterman might have uttered something similar when he jumped on the popemobile to shield John Paul II from any additional bullets. Would-be assassin Mehmet Ali Agca already had hit JP2 in St. Peter's Square on May 13, 1981, but Esterman's subsequent actions earned special notice in the eulogy he received from Vatican secretary of state Cardinal Angelo Sodano. According to recent reports, Esterman and his wife were murdered by a lone nut, a 23 year old vice corporal in the Swiss guard named Cedric Tornay. The story goes that Tornay was distraught about not receiving an award. Now the *Berlin Kurier*, a German newspaper, reports that Esterman began spying on the pope for East Germany that very year, after having contacted him as early as 1979. After killing his superior officer and wife, Tornay ostensibly shot and killed himself. The implications and permutations of these deaths have yet to be analyzed, but the family of Cedric Tornay has already claimed that the Vatican is with-olding the whole truth.

UNIFIED CONSPIRACY
THEORY FOR THE LATE 90S:

Richard Sauder, author of *Underground Tunnels and Bases*, surfaced a report that the late Commerce secretary Ron Brown owned a patent for an AIDS-like retro-virus. In his role as a GATT negotiator, Brown worked to consolidate patents under one global system. A business associate of Brown's, a man named Ferrat, died on Flight 800. Initial reports about the 800 crash warned people away from the rescue area because of the possible existence of AIDS-tainted blood packets. The medical personnel who suggest (courtesy of the Scaife-connected reporter Chris Ruddy) that Brown's skull may have been penetrated by a .45 calibre bullet, work for the Armed Forces Institute of Pathology. That office recently found RNA residue of the 1918 Spanish flu epidemic from the long-buried body of the Inupiat Eskimo. A similar team of Canadian scientists, headed by a man described as a former classmate of Adnan Khashoggi, recovered similar residue from bodies in Norway. Khashoggi is the uncle of Dodie Fayed and architect of the al-Yamama defense contract umbrella—which embodies the Cripple Factor discussed in the essay above—that recently was expanded to include biochemical firms. Word has also recently reached *Steamshovel* that a Dr. Lo, also of the Armed Forces Institute of Pathology, owns a patent on *mycoplasma fermentans incognitus*, a microbe thought by some to cause Gulf War Syndrome.

STEAMSHOVEL PRESS

MATT DRUDGE MEETS THE OCTOPUS

This interesting bit of information about the Drudge/Blumenthal entanglement recently emerged in the *Wall Street Journal* : "When the dispute arose, Mr. Horowitz — whose Center for the Study of Popular Culture is funded in part by Richard Scaife, a fiercely anti-Clinton heir to the Mellon fortune — had just published an autobiography that assailed Mr. Blumenthal for making 'malicious personal attacks' as a journalist. He heard about the Drudge situation from Barbara Ledeen, a Washington acquain-  tance who says she is still "foaming at the mouth" because of stories Mr. Blumenthal wrote about her husband, a former Reagan administration official, and his colleagues. Mr. Horowitz then phoned the young reporter and offered help." ("Drudge Libel Suit Puts Mavens of Free Speech in Awkward Spot," by Edward Felsenthal, *WSJ*, 3/11/98.) The former Reagan official mentioned here is Michael Ledeen, identified by Danny Casolaro as in the periphery of the cabal he sought to expose, the Octopus. Ledeen's covert work and his role in the Center for Strategic and International Studies has been examined at length in Robin Ramsay's *Lobster*.

REICH TEASER

Kenn Thomas has a sidebar to a long article on Reich in a recent issue of *Fortean Times* (107, February 1998). The American edition of that issue has Reich on the cover with sexualized headlines ("Brick Teaser"; "Are Your Horny?", etc.); the UK edition has none of that, only Lionel Fanthorpe on a Harley. Neil Mortimer's article on Reich is a historical summary with interesting graphix work by Etienne Gilfallen. Unfortunately, it totally misses the British angle to Reich's story, notably the role played by Lew Douglas, US embassador to England. Does all this carry a subliminal message that Reich can be marketed best to sex-crazed Americans? *Steamshovel* resists calling this distortion, even though the list of speakers at FT's Uncon this year includes Ian Simmons, who previously has written distorted Reichian history for the magazine. Why isn't Thomas speaking? One clue might be found somewhere in the middle of the list of themes for the UnCon this year "Cults, Conspiracy and Cryptozoology."

ANTHRAX ATTACKS/RIFE STRIFE

Readers following the anthrax-terror arrests in Las Vegas must, as usual, read through the news to get to the bottom of it. Even some of the conspiracy net chatters and web pages have missed a big point—the connection to Rife technology. In the 1930s, Dr. Royal Raymond Rife created a nuclear magnetic resonance plasma beam vacuum tube which can be tuned to destroy cancer and disease cells. Ronald Rockwell, who finked on Larry Wayne Harris and his Mormon ex-bishop patron, William Leavitt, is heir to Rife's work. Rockwell gained this distinction after a death-bed agreement with John Crane, the co-author of a book that revived interest in Rife in 1987. Leavitt apparently offered Rockwell $20m for some latter-day version of the Rife resonance technology. *Steamshovel* recently learned that Leavitt also is represented by Lamond Mills, the same ex-U.S. Attorney who represented by Bo Gritz in the late 1980s.

That's a stiff price tag for a 1930s cancer cure that many argue cannot possibly work. Why would Rockwell turn it down? When linked with modern magnetic resonance technology (what MRIs are made of), promoters of the Rife device say it has the potential to treat anthrax infection en masse, with rooms full of people, maybe even military troops. Coincidentally, the latest issue of *Nexus* (Vol 5, #2, 2-3/98)—issued before the arrests—includes an article on Royal Raymond Rife and his work by a chiropractor who has modernized it.

The news media identify Rockwell simply as a Las Vegas businessman who claimed to have invented a new technology designed to electronically neutralize dangerous toxins without the use of pharmaceuticals or vaccines. Harris and Leavitt were on their way to a public forum in Florida to discuss this when the FBI picked them up. Harris, of course, previously had been arrested for possession of freeze-dried bubonic plague.

A longer article on this by Kenn Thomas will appear in a future issue of *Fortean Times.*

WACO UFO CONNECTION

In Waco, TX, Jason Leigh, a well-known UFO researcher, surrendered Sunday evening, March 8 in Waco, TX, after a 12 hour standoff involving his concern over the plights of US veterans. Leigh took footage of UFO in Roswell a couple of years ago and has been consulted by many research groups and media outlets, including the *Sightings* program. Last summer, while covering the 50th anniversary of Roswell, the folks at *ParaScope* invited Leigh out to its makeshift compound at the Roswell County Fairgrounds. See the *ParaScope* site for an upcoming report.

Quotable: *"I've got to do something to save this guy. He's an intelligent guy. He's got terrible weaknesses, but so does most of his generation, so — you know, why pick on him?"* — Lyndon LaRouche on Bill Clinton

RALLY TO END SECRECY
October 24th 1999 at Noon
Steps of the Capitol Building
Washington DC
http://www.endsecrecy.com

America is America because it's in a state of perpetual revolution. It has learned over the years to absorb every extreme into its mainstream culture. Individuality is praised while slogans like "dare to be different are the kudos of its media campaigns. Our Constitution has allowed us such a luxury. But no massive paradigm shift takes place in this country until or unless its people assemble in sufficient numbers in Washington DC. That's liberty and true democracy in action. It was the case for the civil liberties movement, demanding an end to the Vietnam war, shutting down nukes, attention for AIDS, all these issues and causes mobilized millions of people on the Mall to tip the scales in favor of reason and common sense. But lately there hasn't been any great catalyst. The Million Man March and the Peacekeepers don't really count. They were more about style than substance.

We,ve all been too busy surfing the web and networking online to realize what we are doing is not working. It's just like being on the phone. So while we weren't paying close attention, the real world outside cyberspace just got worse. It's as if America has left the rest of the world behind in its cultural evolution, and now we,re faced with an international order controlling our politicians and our corporations, wanting to bring America down because the secrets we keep scare them. And rightly so

Strange things are flying in our skies. Rumors of extraordinary technologies, louder than X-Files fiction, can no longer be brushed off as wishful thinking. It's come to our realization that what we were fighting for back in the 60s, 70s & 80s was just the tip of the iceberg, that military secrets run deeper and darker than we dared possible. We couldn't or wouldn't admit the truth to ourselves; our government had run away from us, and created its own parallel universe to the tune of billions of tax payer dollars, quietly funneled into black budgets, building underground cities all over the world.

It wouldn't be quite so dramatic if by doing so, the Powers That Be and the Status Quo weren't perpetuating an oil-based economy damaging the very air we breathe at the expense of all life on earth. Ever since Earth Day 1970 the environmental movement has been up against a foe, an enemy, an obstacle, call it what you will, which we,ve never been able to identify. A resistance running deep as an undercurrent against change, which to all should have simply been self-evident. But there was more to it than met the eye. Not only did the financial temptation of keeping the old machinery oiled and running have the upper hand, but a quasi-religious attachment to post-industrial philosophy has prevented serious change at the root base of the problem. It's even visible in the lore of so-called "free energy" or "new energy" advocates who see in a turn-of-the-century hero like Nikola Tesla a future that never was instead of a possible one. They celebrate his forgotten inventions instead of following the money and paper trail that could lead to where they might be today.

Over 10.000 scientific documents are classified every day. It would come to no surprise for most of us to know that since all these technologies are kept under wraps for their destructiveness, along with them disappear their beneficial potential. It's not far fetched to wonder if a great part of our environmental, or medical problems, didn't already have their solutions built into those problems before they were so methodically suppressed. It is to that end that the entire National Security Act has come into scrutiny by some members of the House and Senate under the leadership of Senator Moynihan.

The Rally To End Secrecy was already in the works when his work came to light. The rally plans are an offshoot from the March For Peaceful Energy that was held last year on the steps of the Capitol Building on October 24th 1998. We want to bring national attention to the fact that secrecy has gotten out of hand and needs to be not only curtailed, but also completely reassessed. In the past, a timid attempt at a rally to end UFO secrecy held in DC was foiled by low turnout. The 50th anniversary celebration at Roswell degenerated into a carnival, thanks to spoilers from the intelligence community who wants to preserve the zany aspect of the UFO community intact. It is after all the perfect cover for testing experimental aircraft.

This is why we are asking you, in the alternative media community, who frequently address issues such as these, to promote, publicize and assist us in building momentum for this event, so that once and for all, those who have kept us in the dark can be made accountable for their motives.

Remy Chevalier, Rally To End Secrecy, endsecrecy@hotmail.com

STEAMSHOVEL PRESS

 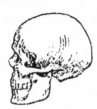

LOREN COLEMAN ON AIDS, CHIMPS AND SASQUATCH

Allow me a moment to take you far from the Patterson Film, which few in the public really care about day to day, to a topic that is on the mind of many around the globe - AIDS. The news today, about the link between chimps and AIDS, could affect cryptozoologists more deeply, in the long-run, than debunkers and hoax claims about the 1967 film. Let me explain:

While the following articles point to humans killing or eating chimpanzees for food as the means by which Homo sapiens got the HIV virus from Pan troglodytes troglodytes, a murky and perhaps absurd question must be raised.

As Dr. Beatrice Hahn has noted, while chimps have long been suspected as the source, "there have been a lot of loose ends that made people uncomfortable drawing that conclusion." Is it an illogical jump that this happened because of sexual contact between chimps and humans? Will this new link be seen as as kind of "open-season" on acquiring chimps for research, vaccines, or worse - or killing them out of fear? And what of gorillas? Or Sasquatch? When Bigfoot is fully discovered, will the then remembered infrequently-reported kidnapping and sexual contact between humans and Oh-Mahs, Ucus and others be blamed for the spread of AIDS?

I think we have to look at such news events as having farflung implications for cryptozoology, on levels we can't even imagine, yet.

STEAMSHOVEL PRESS

HIV ORIGIN IS LINKED TO CHIMPS
FINDING MAY BE STEP TOWARD
DEVELOPMENT OF VACCINE

Chicago Tribune, 1 February 1999

In a finding that helps resolve the longstanding mystery of how the virus that causes AIDS first infected humans, a team of researchers announced on Sunday that the major strain of the virus almost certainly came from a type of African chimpanzee.

The results may one day yield insight into why chimpanzees do not get ill from the simian form of the virus, while the human strains are deadly.

In addition, the findings should help scientists understand how HIV developed and continues to mutate in infected people. Such knowledge is a necessary step toward the elusive goal of fashioning vaccines for the ever-changing virus, experts said.

"If we know where we've been, we can tell where we're going," said Steven Wolinsky, an AIDS researcher at Northwestern University Medical School.

Although many scientists have suggested that the virus was passed to humans from animals, until now there was no convincing proof that chimpanzees were the source, according to Dr. Beatrice Hahn, of the University of Alabama-Birmingham, who led the researchers and who addressed the Conference on Retroviruses and Opportunistic Infections at the Chicago Sheraton.

"We never knew for sure whether (the source) was chimps or another species," said Hahn, noting that monkeys and apes also had been proposed as the source of the epidemic. "Now we know it was the chimps."

Exactly how the virus jumped from chimp to humans remains a mystery, though Hahn proposes that humans originally were infected while hunting chimps for food in Central Africa.

Hahn's discovery of HIV's primate origins began with a chimp named Marilyn.

A research animal taken from an unknown location in Africa in 1959, Marilyn died in 1985 after giving birth to stillborn twins. She tested positive for the simian form of HIV, one of a handful of chimpanzees ever to show signs of contracting the virus naturally.

But laboratory techniques available at the time could not isolate Marilyn's virus, Hahn said. So parts of Marilyn's body were frozen and sent to Dr. Larry Arthur, a researcher at the National Cancer Institute Laboratory at Ft. Detrick, Md.

"He stuffed it in his freezer and it sat there for 10 years. Then one day he had to clean out his freezer, and he found this big bag of chimpanzee parts. He knew about my research, so he called me." said Hahn, who was studying the primate origins of HIV.

"On occasion you get lucky," she said.

Using polymerase chain reaction (PCR), a method of amplifying traces of genetic material that became widespread only after 1985, Hahn's team was able to isolate Marilyn's virus and compare it with three other samples of the HIV-like virus that infects chimpanzees, identified as SIVcpz, shorthand for simian immuno virus from chimpanzees.

The results, to be published in this week's issue of the journal Nature, showed that Marilyn's virus was closely related to strains found in two other primates belonging to the chimpanzee subspecies Pan troglodytes troglodytes, which were taken from the Central African country of Gabon.

Those strains also were similar to HIV-1, the most common strain of the virus that afflicts humans. HIV-1 is thought to have originated among humans in the same region of Central Africa that forms the natural range of Marilyn's subspecies. The fourth infected chimp, which had a very different form of SIVcpz, belonged to a different chimpanzee subspecies native to East Africa.

Statistical tests indicated that Marilyn's form of the virus and the two samples taken from the Gabon chimps formed a common genetic lineage with HIV-1. Those varieties of chimp virus are more similar to the human virus than they are to the virus taken from the East African chimp subspecies.

Previous research by Hahn and others already had shown that the less common human strain of HIV-2 had its source in sooty mangabeys, a monkey often kept as a pet in West Africa.

Additional genetic tests convinced Hahn that humans living in Central Africa contracted HIV-1 from the chimp subspecies to which Marilyn belongs.

"She filled in the blanks, the missing links," said Douglas Richman, a researcher at the University of California at San Diego and head of the retrovirus conference where Hahn gave her paper Sunday.

Northwestern's Wolinsky co-authored an article in the journal Science last year that used genetic techniques to conclude that HIV first entered the human population sometime between 1927 and 1942. It's possible that chimps passed on the virus during that time span, though Wolinsky said the connection cannot yet be proved.

Because the simian virus taken from the two chimp subspecies is so different, Hahn thinks it may have been present in chimpanzees even before the chimp groups diverged, several hundred thousand years ago.

That leaves open the mystery of why HIV became a widespread human problem only in the last few decades, infecting up to 30 million people worldwide.

However the virus was spread, Wolinsky said it's probably no coincidence that the rise of HIV has occurred just as humans have increased trade through parts of Africa that are home to the chimpanzee.

That's dangerous for chimpanzees whose habitats are being destroyed, and for humans who may be exposed to new diseases.

"As contacts with animals in these areas become more common, these events might occur more often," Wolinsky said.

steamshovel press

CAROL ROSIN ON
CLINTON MILITARY BUILDUP

Carol Rosin vitae: Founder, Institute for Security and Cooperation in Outer Space, ISCOS First woman exec in an aerospace industry Spokesperson for the late Dr. Wernher von Braun Space and missile defense consultant who helped start the movement to ban weapons from space, who started the "the Leaky Umbrella Campaign," the "SOS-Save Outer Space" Campaign, etc..: "Rosin is regarded to be the original political architect of the movement to stop the SDI and ASAT's," a quote from "Military Space" magazine. Testified numerous times before the Congress about this issue.

From the mailbag of *Stop Cassini:* Carol Rosin responds (#1)

To: "Russell D. Hoffman" <rhoffman@animatedsoftware.com From: carol rosin <rosin@west.net Subject: Re: 16th Happy Symposium on the wonderful uses of space nuclear power and propulsion... STOP CASSINI #87 February 1st, 1999

#87 is pretty funny to me. I mean truly laughable. Puts a sick smile on my face.

Here's my answer to a question that an author we know just asked me about...why the media didn't cover the funding of the Star Wars and related programs that just happened.

This answer is relevant to all this, really:

Note, this is what I've been telling you would happen if WE didn't take a position from the beginning to first ban all space-based weapons instead of focusing on the nuclear issues: We have now witnessed the first tier of the Star Wars space-based weapons system funded. And, the media completely missed the fact that Clinton made an important trade-off which allows him to stay in office in return for his support for the first phase of the Star Wars funding and a few wars thrown in. Yes, everybody is happy now. You remember that candidate who promised that if elected he'd stop Star Wars. Well, what's one more lie...it just got missed, so what.

Of course, this whole story of the Clinton trade-off slid by the media. Hidden perfectly. No protest. And the spin masters call it something other than what it really is. They add that it isn't what Reagan really wanted (though in reality, it is the first part of it...soon to build momentum so that none of it can be stopped). It must be so utterly boring to the media (no sex, no blood and guts, yet) that while it did hit the news, they barely notice that it is often called a Ballistic Missile Defense System or a Global Protection System instead of a Strategic Defense Initiative. They say it isn't the Star Wars program as Reagan called for. And, either the public believes them, or wants it, or doesn't care...not because of a media error, but because of the lack of information, misinformation, ignorance or apathy.

We all know Clinton lies, and we all know he is now tied into this space-based weapon system that is absolutely unnecessary, unworkable, destabalizing, unwanted, untestible, dangerous, draining, and too costly...and won't stop a suitcase bomb or a bacteria warfare. Yet, there is no outcry when it is funded ... those who do know about it are afraid to lose their jobs or are desperate for funding so they will support anything as long as they get the money.

Though we have only a teenie window of opportunity in which we could steer things easily into a direction that most everyone would love instead of into this one that will kill us all, the war game on earth has now officially been escalated into space...funding-wise.

You see, there isn't anything new that is really attractive to the media. There is no dramatic or creative talk of how we could transform the war game of technologies and mindsets, the old game, into a space game with the highest of technologies and consciousness... without losing any jobs or profits.

If there was any talk at all to the media, it has mostly been centered on the stopping of underground nuclear testing, the stopping of the Cassini mission, or on other secondary bandaids related to the nuclear issue.

Sometimes those who protested said they were against the militarization of space...even though space is already militarized and even though the military has a totally different role in space that benefits us all...IF we don't put weapons in space. The foundation, the premise upon which all this was happening, the weaponization of space, was confused as it was presented to the media, at best, and at worst was put on the back burner as an issue. There has been nothing new, recently, in the space conversation that would attract the media to this story...except the funding that has been recently allotted.

The media would have been attracted if a worldwide movement had begun to ban all space-based weapons...to sign a verifiable treaty to ban all weapons in space. This movement, which would call for the ban while simultaneously calling for an expanded world cooperative space program to replace the war industry, would have caused the media to take notice and to track the space related nuclear issue in a unique way...to focus on alternatives instead of on the usual anti-nuke protests.

But, the nuclear protestors who took on the space issue didn't want to take on the space issue as a primary issue...and so they became part of the old game that always did fit. Protests and reactions to what the military industrial complex produced.

Unfortunately, these protesters could seem to relate to a positive vision...the one that showed how we could/can create a healthy and prosperous planet with more jobs and profits, more products and services, a stimulated economy with a real security system based on cooperative world space military, civilian and commercial technologies and services that would provide an abundance of unlimited benefits and opportunities to all the world's peoples. We could apply these services and technologies directly to solve our earthbound problems...including those of the environment, humans and other animals...as we evolve into the universes. All of this can only be created by transforming the war game into a space game. But, just as there are vested interests in the nuclear and weapons industry, there are vested interests in those who work to try to "stop" them.

It doesn't surprise me one bit that there is no media attention. Once ISCOS, the only group who focused only on this space weapons and alternatives issue including on the stimulation of relevant action disappeared, and got NO recognition or support from those who supposedly care about this issue, the "egos" rose to the surface to give their speeches and sell their books mostly about why nukes in space are a bad thing. Most of the "peace in space" activists, the handful of them, bumped each other out of the limelight with their infighting. Why would the media be attracted to this? No wonder the media wasn't interested. They have plenty of hot issues to cover.

The media has been given little or no information except from a small few authors and so-called experts...hardly enough to attract or maintain their attention. There are no dramatic coalition statements to make and no individuals working with the high level decision makers who are at the helm ... and so the small and splintered coalition doesn't attract any media attention or even educate them.

Of course, there are the scientist groups and a few peace groups who continue to say they are against space weapons and the nuclear technogies they deem dangerous while they compromise in their positions, as they lie to their subscribers about what they are REALLY going for in the Congress...taking compromised positions so that they will "look credible" and be "politically effective," neither of which they are. Then there are the space advocates pushing for commercial and civilian ventures in legislation, not acknowledging the inexorable link to the military ventures ... in fact, never never mentioning "space-based weapons" for fear of losing their funding or jobs. And, I mean, 12 people protesting on a launch pad ... people who never did see the whole picture and, therefore, didn't call for the priority issue (a ban on space-based weapons...which would have put a literal lid on all this and would have called for a new way of thinking entirely) ... well, gimmie a break. Why would the media cover such a weak picture.

Finally we see, WAG THE DOG style, the truth that isn't being addressed ... more wars to cover-up what is really going on plus Clinton trading space weapons funding for being able to remain in his seat. The media, and most everyone, missed this completely. The trade-off Clinton made...with the lack of media attention, is what makes me realize it's about time to throw in the towel. There is no awakening ... no shift in consciousness or awareness...and we are all about to die...geeze, I used to be such a positive person.... But, clearly, this story was completely missed by the media...and, how could they know about it?

This trade-off, more weapons, now the first tier of space weapons being funded midst the wars and the cigars, was not noticed by the media. The rest of the story is old news. This is the new news that should have hit the media fan. The media doesn't seem to realize that the space weapons funding so satisfies the Republicans that they will do their Senate hearings (mainly to satisfy their media image and constituents) but that there is no need, now, to replace him. Now, the Democrats and the Republicans are the same...all want to tear down the forests, have lots of wars so we can further build what is already the largest R&D program in recorded history, the space-based weapons program...well, hmmmm, they are non-partisan on one issue. They are all now committed to continuing the destruction and suffering on earth by escalating the arms race into space...always to "seize the high ground." This could include an escalation of dangerous nuclear technologies...as the mindset hasn't changed one bit. As was said in a strategy paper I submitted, years ago, to Congress as a supplement to one of my Congressional testimonies on this issue, words I found that were designed by the Heritage Foundation, included our USA intention to "steal the language of the arms control community" as they build this space-based weapon system "regardless of the merits or non-merits of the system." In other words, the trade-off gets lost in the news intentionally, and almost everyone gets what they want. At least, that's how the media must be seeing it. They sure aren't seeing any protest or new suggestions.

With the lack of media attention and public action, it won't surprise me at all when we very soon shall see our bodies and environment continue to break down, and soon will see our children's faces melt, due to lack of intelligent attention and funding on important issues as brains and money get further dedicated to developing this next phase of unlimited extended warfare into that place above all our heads. If we survive much longer, we'll get a chance to see hundreds of battlestations with thousands of weapons pointed down our throats. Meanwhile, we'll be satisfied with the usual crumbs, called "spin-offs," of the war gamers. So, why would the media be attracted to this story? Boring.

The sex and war stories are humorous and dramatic. The public laps them up, while claiming they aren't interested. The world laughs at the US media, but the world media, too, has nothing more to project. We've got zillions of channels on TV to turn to if we don't like these stories, to fill our minds. Space ... so what ... there are plenty of movies about it that are similar to the real life ones.

Until we, who understand that we can have peace on earth through peace in space, that we can survive in harmony and love in the light, by becoming aware of what can be done only right NOW to ban weapons from space and to build world cooperative space military, civilian and commercial ventures...until we focus on this with all our hearts and minds on educating the media about what space is all about (not just to build commercial ventures or just to build Star Wars)...we deserve to get little or no media coverage.

If we do something dramatic, build a movement about transforming the military industrial complex and relationships around the world (without threatening jobs, politics or the economy...and with stimulating all of them in a most positive way), until we reach the decision makers with what is feasible that we want in our space frontier that will benefit all of us, until we call for a worldwide ban on all space-based weapons and simultaneously for ideas from everyone of all ages around the world about what we can do in space together ... we won't get the kind of media attention space deserves.

Listen, I could go public about the [men] I slept with while I worked in Washington. But, at this point, that story is told. It's done. We all know this part, now. This story is just more of the same. What's exciting about the media saturating the world with this story is that now, maybe now, the people of the world will be more receptive to a brand new story that will stimulate them with even more sex appeal and fun.

Look at it this way, Clinton has given us a gift...this cover-up/trade-off story. It's certainly a complex, exciting, sexy, dramatic, humorous story worthy of media attention. It's riveted the world. And, best of all, we should now be able to see that the media might just want to see this next level of truth...the trade-off...and how it leads us into an entirely new way of thinking...a cosmic way. We've linked the world to this story. Now, with the space issue emerging in the middle of it, if we raise the issue...the world might just grasp it and start an entire movement to cause a huge change that would allow our species and many others to survive and relish in the Space Age together on this Earth. And, the media who "get it," who help bring the space piece to the awareness of the world public and decision makers, would also help us get the word out...about the importance of cooperative space R&D to our survival on earth! Don't you think the media would love to participate in telling a story like this one? From the mailbag: Carol Rosin responds (#2)

This newsletter content doesn't surprise me at all. I've been trying to tell everyone that if we don't ban weapons from space as our primary focus...and stop trying to stop these nuclear tests and launches (or at least put them as a secondary issue), we won't stop the industry from putting either weapons or nukes in space. But no, no one would listen. The "coalition" of anti-nuke activists do it again...lose. It's kinda like going to a surgeon...if you go to a surgeon, they recommend surgery. If you gather anti-nuclear types, you get a focus on nukes. Unfortunately, from one who came out of the military industrial complex strategy department, that isn't the game they are playing. They are playing the game of going into space...and nukes are only a small part of it. They'll hide the rest by focusing the public and Congressional eyes on the civilian and commercial uses...and the experts in that field are "afraid" to mention, let alone be against, nuclear technologies in space. Their jobs and funding are at stake. Meanwhile, just as I thought, we're going to have lots of weapons and nuclear technologies in that space above all our heads. Why? Because even though there is a TEENIE window open of opportunity in which we could get the word out, the Coalition Against the Weaponization and Nuclearization of Space fits their protest perfectly into the game by continuing to emphasize the WRONG protest and NO solutions that are realistic. I mean, these are the same people who think we should build roads and schools instead of guns...duh. That ain't where the industry is headed...wrong argument, again. As usual, nothing new is vote or media worthy coming from the so-called coalition who have their hearts in the right place but who have their egos confused with their minds and their old way of thinking and acting. And so, the game goes on as usual. Just a bit of sex scandles and more wars to cover-up...WAG THE DOG style. And the game simply accelerates as it escalates into the space frontier. Guess I'll go to my grave not wanting to say outloud, "I told you so."

Will our group wake up? Doubtful. Too busy selling their anti-nuclear books and protesting nukes. Too bad. We could have banned all weapons from the space frontier, thus CAUSING another way of "THINKING" to emerge.

But since WE don't allow our spirits to guide us rather than our egos, we continue the fight in the same earthbound way against issues that will not be dented, without incorporating a cosmic consciousness, without putting a literal lid on the reasons we "need" nukes in space, and without calling for worldwide space military, commercial and civilian space cooperative R&D and ventures that could have taken us, Akido style, into the millennium in a way worthy of the Space Age.

So, I think it's time to focus on whatever makes you happy in life. We are all going to die sooner than we thought. And these words come from a former optimist. AND IN CONCLUSION...

Do we all feel better now? Safer, more at ease? Do we feel like we've done enough for our children, and our children's children, today? Have we served the human race to the best of our ability? Pass this newsletter on. There is someone out there who has not read it.

Please send any news directly to the editor at the email address given below. Please feel free to post these newsletters anywhere you feel it's appropriate! You can send them to news media too! (If possible, please do not send or post these newsletters anonymously.) THANKS!!!

Welcome new subscribers!

Thanks for reading,

Sincerely, Russell D. Hoffman rhoffman@animatedsoftware.com Editor STOP CASSINI Newsletter Webmaster STOP CASSINI Web Site http://www.animated-software.com/cassini/cassini.htm

CANCEL CASSINI

ARLEN WILSON PASSES

Arlen Wilson, wife of *Illuminatus!* author Robert Anton Wilson, died peacefully in her sleep on May 22. RAW says "don't worry about me." *Steamshovel* shares in the grief over the passing of this great woman.

MCKENNA MEDICAL WORRY

According to Art Bell, Terrence McKenna has a brain tumor. Terrence had a seizure and was airlifted to a hospital, suffering cardiac arrest in transit, like Richard Hoagland. The report described a 1 inch by 2.5 centimeter tumor in a frontal lobe. Bell initated a prayer effort, which is also the way Bell does "cloudbusting."

FEATHER COSTUME CONTRIBUTED TO WRESTLER'S DEATH

Kansas City investigators report that a feathered costume may have caused a cable to malfunction, initiating the fall that killed Owen Hart, a wrestler for the WWF. Other rumors include suggestions of murder by dominance-degradation elements among WWF executive elements. The 34-year-old Hunt plummetted 90-feet from the top Kemper Arena in Kansas City on May 23. Kansas City police say feathers from Hart's A quick release mechanism jammed on a harness holding the wrestler because of  the feathers. The harness was to lower Hart into the ring, as part of an effort to humiliate him. Dominance, degradation, humiliation—themes that help explain recent affiliation between the wrestling world and politics.

SUPREME COURT LETS
MORROW VERDICT STAND

In 1989 the *Globe* tabloid newspaper reprinted charges made by former CIA agent Robert Morrow that Pakistani native Khalid Khawar (named Ali Ahmand by Morrow) assassinated Robert Kennedy with a gun disguised as a camera, on behalf of the shah of Iran. Morrow made the claim in his 1988 book, *The Senator Must Die*. Khawar filed a defamation suit that ended with a $1,175,000 award. The California Supreme Court upheld the judgement last year and on May 17, the US Supreme Court let the verdict stand "without comment or dissent." The decision ignored arguments by the *Globe*'s lawyers that the case "seriously threatens the right of the media to accurately report previously published allegations of public concern"—which would include book reviews as well as news items based on controversial books—should be protected against libel lawsuits.

HITCHENS, KOESTLER AND REICH

In a brief conversation outside the Midnight Special bookstore in Los Angeles, critic Christopher Hitchens offered his opinion that recent charges of rape made against the renown anti-Communist and paranormalist Arthur Koestler (pictured at left) are true. Apparently Hitchens knows one of the accusers, Jill Craigie, and does not doubt her word. Craigie's word includes the detail that she had forced Koestler out of her building, let him back in and then the rape occurred. Hitchens noted that he has recently finished a column about this and *Steamshovel* looks forward to his full analysis.

Mr. Hitchens had a brush with high notoriety (although already rightfully well-known and respected) a few weeks ago when he reported that he heard the story about Monica Lewinsky stalking Clinton from Sydney Blumenthal, the White House conspiracy theorist (known as "GK" for "Grassy Knoll"). Clinton once told Blumenthal that he felt trapped, like the character Rubashov in Arthur Koestler's novel, *Darkness At Noon*. Interestingly, in a recent column for *The Nation*, Mr. Hitchens mentions that one of the Serb anti-fascist internationalists he stays in contact with is Dusan Makavejev, the filmmaker responsible for *WR-Mysteries of the Organism*, a fairly wretched misfire of a documentary (identified by Hitchens as "one of the defining movies of the seventies") that nevertheless contains the only available footage of Wilhelm Reich. At one time, Reich and Koestler shared a red cell.

steamshovel press

LITTLE LETTER FROM THE UK

Lobster's Robin Ramsay sent this missive: Hull, Tuesday Dear Kenn, There's a book out about the Rhodes scholars: *Cowboys into Gentlemen,* (sic!) *Rhodes Scholars, Oxford and the Creation of an American Elite* by Thomas J. Schaeper and Kathleen Schaeper (Berghahn Books, NY and Oxford, 1998). Not a very good book, though full of interesting fragments on US Rhodies. In chapter 15 the authors consider the conspiracy theories around Rhodies, miss out Quigley! but say this on p 338: "Most of the leading exponents of this conspiracy theory are little known to the general public, but they have thousands of devoted fanatical fellow-believers. From the late 1940s to the present day they have churned out thousands (??? -RR) of books and newsletters claiming to provide incontrovertible proof of their charges. Two of the most famous books are Rose L. Martin's *Fabian Freeway: High Road to Socialism in the USA* (1989) and Gary Allen's *None Dare Call it Conspiracy* (1971). One of the more influential periodicals espousing these views is aptly titled *Steamshovel.*" The aptly bit I don't get ...old fashioned? Heavy industry? Blue collar? Best, Robin

Above: *Steamshovel*'s Kenn Thomas, ready to heave some heavy industry at Schaeper and Schaeper.

STEAMSHOVEL PRESS

HALLELLUJAH HAROLD WEISBERG!

Kris Millegan reminded *Steamshovel Press* to take some space to celebrate the achievement of Harold Weisberg, long-time luminary of JFK research. In April, Harold and his wife Lil reached their 86th and 87th birthdays. Weisberg wrote the *Whitewash* series and the assassination. He has otherwise been an articulate spokesman for the truth and a guiding light in the social/political darkness of the decades that followed the assassination. *Steamshovel* wishes the Weisbergs many more happy years, secure in the knowledge that their contribution is known, has been understood and the US—bad as it may be—is a better place because of them. Genuine heros! Please send cards and letters of love to them at 7627 Old Receiver Road, Frederick, MD 21702.

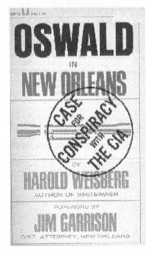

OSWALD
IN
NEW ORLEANS
CASE FOR CONSPIRACY WITH THE CIA
HAROLD WEISBERG
AUTHOR OF WHITEWASH
FOREWORD BY
JIM GARRISON
DIST. ATTORNEY, NEW ORLEANS

STEAMSHOVEL PRESS

STILL SHROUDED

Skeptics want to conclude that Carbon 14 tests already performed on the Shroud of Turin conclusively prove it to be a medieval forgery. Not so says organic chem prof James S. Chickos. Introduction of molten silver and water from the effort to combat a fire suffered by the supposed burial cloth of Jesus contaminated the sample, as many have pointed out. Chickos, however, has another angle: chemical changes in the linen through the introduction of long carbon chains

found in lipids from the tallow in candles found on the shroud. "Our hypothesis is that the tallow from candle wax reacted chemically with the glucose to produce an ester of cellulose, thereby adding to the carbon base," says Chickos.

CASTRATION FRUSTRATION

The March 1998 issue of *American Journal of Psychiatry* includes an interesting case history of a self-declared "monk" who requested castration because his sexual impulses interfered with his spirituality. The oblate thought that "castration was the final and best option to ablate his sexuality." The consulting psychiatrist concluded that the request was legit, long-standing and non-psychotic, but denied the request and treated the patient instead with a gonadotropin-releasing hormone analogue. Two years later the "monk" joined Heaven's Gate and offed himself.

FATE REVIEWS *STEAMSHOVEL*

From the May 1999 issue of *FATE*:

Flying Saucers Over Los Angeles: The UFO Craze of the '50s DeWayne B. Johnson and Kenn Thomas, from Adventures Unlimited Press Softcover, 1998, 280 pgs., $16.00. Also available through The Book Tree (800) 700-TREE

Ever notice how books written years ago often make for more satisfying reading than the bulk of what is being churned out today? This seems to be true particularly when it comes to UFOS. Nostalgics will be delighted with *Flying Saucers Over Los Angeles*, a previously unpublished student dissertation written by DeWayne B. Johnson in 1950. Kenn Thomas (pictured at right), editor of *Steamshovel Press*, stumbled on this valuable historical document while researching the controversial Maury Island affair.

The well-researched manuscript contains reports from 1947-1950, a time when America's skies seemed infested with UFOS. Johnson focuses on Los Angeles in 1950, before the flurry of saucer books published from the mid-1950s through the 1960s.

Of particular note is information Johnson gleaned from a friendly United Press International correspondent about Kenneth Arnold, whose 1947 "flying saucer" sighting near Mt. Rainier kicked off the modern era in ufology. These early interviews with Arnold portray him as a paranoid man, irrationally worried about hidden microphones, who believed the saucers were somehow connected to a rash of mystery submarine reports off the U.S. coast.

Johnson presents an impartial face as he seeks explanations, giving consideration to hoaxes, secret government projects, extraterrestrial theories, and psychosocial factors. Debunkers have their say, no matter how convoluted their logic. One Australian physiologist, for example, endorses the idea that UFO reports are caused by the effect of "red corpuscles ... passing in front of the retina."

Flying Saucers Over Los Angeles is lavishly illustrated with vintage saucer material and an eye-popping color section of archival *FATE* covers and UFO photos. UFO historians will treasure this superb chronology of the events that marked the beginning of ufology.

- Peter Jordan

THE TIPPIT CONNECTION

Steamshovel Press

Warren Commission counsel David Belin called the murder of Officer Tippit the "Rosetta Stone" of the case against Lee Harvey Oswald as the assassin of President John Kennedy. If you accept that Oswald shot Tippit, then you accept that he also shot the President. Indeed, the Tippit murder falls under the 'motive' section of the report.

Belin's perspective seems to always be the mirror-reverse of reality. He steadfastly opposed any possibility of anything than what is in the Warren Commission report. He adamantly refused to concede even the smallest mistakes for fear that once compromised, his grand project - the report - might crumble. Belin would go to great lengths to avoid erosion. His consistent inflexibility is obvious proof of the weakness of the work. Why did he have to spend the thirty six years after its release trying to convince people of the accuracy (mainly by repeating its conclusions ad nauseum) of his report? His purpose, his fear, should have been unwarranted if his efforts were honest.

His Rosetta Stone analogy is true in that the Tippit murder is the small, coded piece that once translated, yields the cipher to the larger puzzle.

The deceptions of the Warren Report can be discovered and resolved in this minor homicide and then applied to the mysteries of the major homicide.

Belin himself may be the true Rosetta Stone of the Warren Report. The key that locks the door shut may be used to open the door as well.

The murder of Tippit was used by the Commission as evidence of motive to prove the killer of Kennedy. The killer is manifestly guilty of murder 'A' because he manifestly committed murder 'B'. The evidence that he committed murder 'B' is that he manifestly committed murder 'A'.

- Such is the logic of the Report

The facts of the case are not limited to the ones presented in the official report.
The key to the code is what isn't there. Belin omits.
Relevancy is the given reason for omission, but relevancy must be
determined by the judge, not the investigator.
Much evidence was not included in the Report. Such as;

A photograph taken by the crime scene photographer of a stop sign
knocked down at the intersection where the officer was shot.
The photographer was told at the scene that it was relevant.

The collection of evidence from the scene includes a strip
of window ledge from,
"which the shots were thought to be fired",
as described by the reporting officer.
But the Report includes no shots fired from any window,
nor any mention of a window ledge.

Tippit had a clipboard in his car that
can be seen in the crime scene photos.
It appears to have a photograph of a
man under its clamp.
But the clipboard nor any information
of what was on it is offered in the
official release of information
of the investigation.

Tippit's murder
was less
documented
than the President's
but also,
less investigated,
and less sensational.

It seems also that the
investigation of it, and
the cover-up of the truth
was less veiled.

This little murder and its facts may hold the keys to the big cryptogram.

The Warren Commission Report could find no connection of any kind between Oswald and Tippit. although Sam Rogers , the manager of the Dobbs House restaurant, two waitresses; Mary Dowling and Dolores Harrison, and another employee; Douglas Leake, all told FBI investigators that Tippit and Oswald were both regular morning customers.

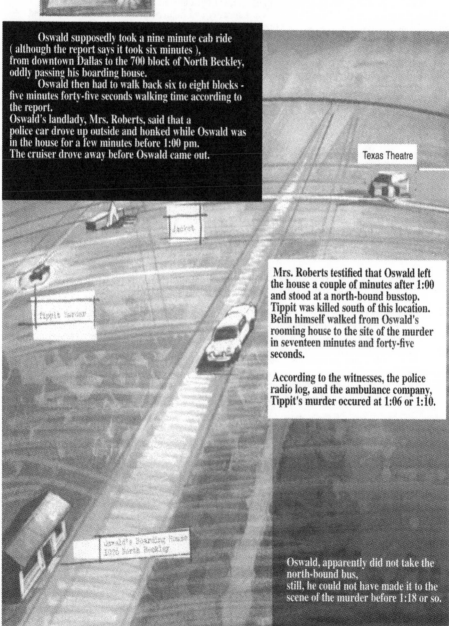

Oswald supposedly took a nine minute cab ride (although the report says it took six minutes), from downtown Dallas to the 700 block of North Beckley, oddly passing his boarding house.

Oswald then had to walk back six to eight blocks - five minutes forty-five seconds walking time according to the report.

Oswald's landlady, Mrs. Roberts, said that a police car drove up outside and honked while Oswald was in the house for a few minutes before 1:00 pm. The cruiser drove away before Oswald came out.

Texas Theatre

Jacket

Tippit Murder

Oswald's Boarding House 1026 North Beckley

Mrs. Roberts testified that Oswald left the house a couple of minutes after 1:00 and stood at a north-bound busstop. Tippit was killed south of this location. Belin himself walked from Oswald's rooming house to the site of the murder in seventeen minutes and forty-five seconds.

According to the witnesses, the police radio log, and the ambulance company, Tippit's murder occured at 1:06 or 1:10.

Oswald, apparently did not take the north-bound bus, still, he could not have made it to the scene of the murder before 1:18 or so.

Fifteen minutes after the shooting of the president in Dealy Plaza, in downtown Dallas, Officers Tippit and Nelson were sent to Oak Cliff, an outlying suburb, by the police radio dispatcher. They were the only two units sent anywhere other than to the scene of the president's assassination. This was also the only exception to a general order for all squads to proceed to the scene downtown, and policeman from districts further away than Tippit's district reported in at Dealy Plaza. Officer Mentzel, who was assigned to the Oak Cliff district that day, was eating lunch within the district at the time of the call. Forty-five minutes after this unique request by the dispatcher, Officer Nelson reported in on the radio at Dealy plaza, as if he had not acknowledged the request to go to Oak Cliff with Tippit. In later years, Nelsonb has offered to sell his story, (since he has never been officially questioned about it) but as of yet there have been no buyers.

Tippit acknowledged nine minutes after the order that he was at Lancaster and Eigth Street in Oak Cliff. He was told then to "be at large for any emergency that comes in".

Sergeant Owens, when asked in Commission testimony why Tippit might have been in Oak Cliff, (without benefit of seeing a transcript of the radio transmissions showing the Tippit and Nelson order) said that Tippit was taking a "logical route" downtown. Commission counsel then established that Owens, (in charge of the Oak Cliff district) and other officers from that district went downtown directly.

At that point testimony went 'off the record'.

At 1:00 the dispatcher tried to get ahold of Tippit, but received no answer.

At 1:08 Tippit tried to contact the dispatcher twice but was not acknowledged.

The source of the description of the suspect in the shooting of the president, aired at 12:44, has never been firmly established. The known witnesses described a man and his clothing but the officer's voice on the radio recordings added the details;
"five-ten, one hundred sixty-five pounds, about thirty years old, and carrying a rifle "

When another officer requests the clothing description again the voice responded,
"The current witness can't remember that".

The witness who said he saw a man in a window above the president's motorcade said that he had seen a man sticking something out of a window. Obviously all that this witness could have provided officers at the scene was perhaps hair and shirt color. Nevertheless the voice recorded on the police radio calls tape repeated the description again adding; "thirty-thirty" to the caliber of the rifle, and changed the "one hundred and sixty pounds" to "slender build".

All of this must be accepted without question in order to base the postulation by the Warren Commission that Tippit was looking for a man that matched the radio description.

All of this must be accepted without question in order to base the postulation by the Warren Commission that Tippit was looking for a man that matched the radio description.

Tippit Assass:
1:10 - 1:16

Just after 1:16 a call went in to the dispatcher from a citizen using a police radio
reporting a shooting of a police officer on Tenth Street in Oak Cliff.
"What location on Tenth?" the dispatcher asked.
"Between Marsalis and Beckley, 404 Tenth Street " replied the citizen.
The dispatcher promptly sent out an APB for
"501 East Jefferson".

Within three minutes and without further information from the radio, the
dispatcher announced the location as
"501 East Tenth ".
When Officers Poe and Jez called and asked if "519 East Jefferson " is correct,
the dispatcher replied, "501 East Jefferson and 501 East Tenth ".

Then after allowing Captain Talbert to blame the citizen for the confusion,and add yet another incorrect, previously un
mentioned street name,"Chesapeake "to the radio audience, the dispatcher then relayed the correct location.

At about 1:20 the dispatcher reported that the suspect had just passed
"401 East Jefferson ".
This location is much closer to where the dispatcher predicted he would be four minutes earlier.

Exhibit No. 20
An artist's reconstruction of the shooting of Officer Tippit.

Nelson called in from downtown to ask if he was needed. The dispatcher sent him to the service station at 4340 West Davis, (near the Tippit slaying) for "info on this suspect. The suspect pulled in there driving a white pontiac station wagon with a rifle in the back seat".

Someone called in to report that he'd found the suspect's jacket in a parking lot behind a service station at 400 East Jefferson. The caller, listed as "#279" in the Warren Commission's evidence is unamed and unknown to the Dallas police department. Officers Westerbrook and Hutson - who are credited with the discovery of the jacket - did not find it and do not know who did

Nelson reported from the service station that two males left the area going east on Davis with a rifle in the back seat. The dispatcher told Nelson to go to 400 East Jefferson and look for that vehicle. Perhaps this is the dispatcher's perogative to call off a pursuit in favor of sending that man to an already over-manned search of an open parking lot, but nevertheless, the dispatcher never repeated the information about a station wagon with two men and a rifle.

Officer McDonald asked for help searching a church at Tenth and Crawford. A witness testified later that he chased a man fleeing the scene into a church. But Officer Walker called in to report that a man ran into the library and squads of policemen went there instead. After the man in the library was discovered to be the wrong man, the search did not return to the church and that information was never mentioned again.

Shortly before Oswald was apprehended, Sergeant Hill called to say that the spent shells found at the scene indicate that the weapon was an automatic. Oswald's revolver is not an automatic.

Oswald, who earlier could move a block a minute according to the Report, now took almost a half an hour to go five blocks. Even though some witnesses said he was running.

Officers were swarming along West Jefferson - the route from the shooting to the Texas Theater - thanks to the trail of shells and clothing and witness-alerting eratic behavior and a radio dispatcher who calls out locations before events happen , yet Oswald was not seen by anyone on that street.

At about 2:30, an APB went out to all squads in the Oak cliff area to pick up for investigation of a CCW (Carrying a Concealed Weapon) the occupants of a 1957 Cheverolet sedan bearing license number NA4445, last seen in the vicinity of tenth and Jefferson.
Since the broadcast mentions "occupants" (plural)- there are more than one person in the car, but it is not the station wagon at the service station,
so that makes two cars and at least four people
with weapons at the scene who have never been found.

At about 1:46 Lee Harvey Oswald
was arrested in the Texas Theater

District Attorney Henry Wade said he is confident of getting the death penalty for Oswald, who is charged also with murder in the shooting of a Dallas policeman.

Dear Earl,
Please empty
this fruitcake

merry christmas
DPD

There is much evidence to show that whoever slipped into the Texas Theater was not arrested. Oswald bought a ticket and went in sometime after 1:00, when the feature's scheduled showtime was, according to the concession usher
Warren Burroughs.

He never saw the man who came in at 1:35.
That man apparently went upstairs to the balcony, since Burroughs could not see the stairs to the balcony from his position at the concession counter. That man also did not buy any popcorn from Burroughs as he says Oswald did when he came in.

Each and every witness to the Tippit shooting had a different version of what happened.
There are about twenty-five witnesses that have been written about, while the Warren Report claims there were either six or twelve. The Report says that three saw the shooting, but actually there were only two. One didn't actually see the shots fired because his view was obscured.

Of the remaining two named by the Report, Mrs Helen Markham, (described by Commission Counsel Ball as an "utter screwball" and "totally unreliable"), had testified so irrationally that the Commission chose only certain parts to use.

The third witness, Domingo Benavides saw the incident from across the street while parked in his truck about fifteen feet away. Surely closer than anyone else, and very reliable as compared to Markham, Benavides didn't go down to ID the suspect because he couldn't "remember the guy well enough".

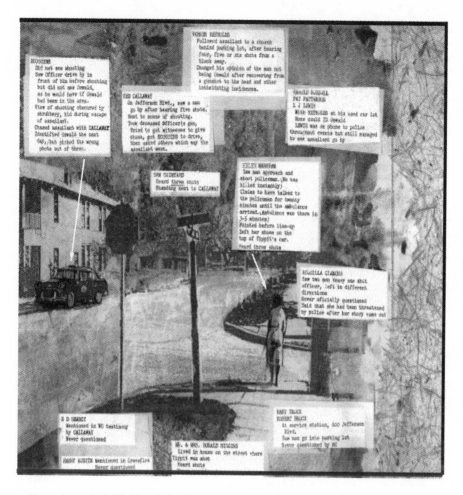

The 'totally unreliable' Markham denied five times recognizing any man in the line-up. Finally agreeing later that "number two" (Oswald) was the man.

The photo of Oswald that had appeared in the national media following the president's assassination was shown to other witnesses that the Commission decided to talk to two months after the incident.
Some of those witnesses said yes it was him and some said no.

Warren Reynolds said that he could not identify the man in the photo. Two days later, he was shot in the head.
He survived and was able to testify six months later that Oswald was the man that he saw that day that the officer was killed.

Moreover, the commission left out many witnesses and much evidence that indicated that two men shot Tippit and that at least one left the scene by car. Also, a number of witnesses that had to be included in the Report to buttress the Commission's theory had evidence that the assailant was coming from the other direction - an impossibility for Oswald.

Mr. and Mrs. Brock, Reynolds, and either Patterson or
Russell watched the parking lot until the police arrived.
Captain Westerbrook and an unknown officer found a
jacket under one of the cars and Sergeant Hill prepared to
search the Abundant Life Temple.

Because of the witnesses on the corner at the service
station, the suspect - if in the parking lot, could not have
gotten across Crawford, or back out to Jefferson.

This promising dragnet lost some of its manpower when
the call to search the library.

(in the other direction on Jefferson) came in.

Sergeant Hill remained at the church, apparently since he
was on foot, and soon gave up on his search when a call
came in that the suspect was at the theater

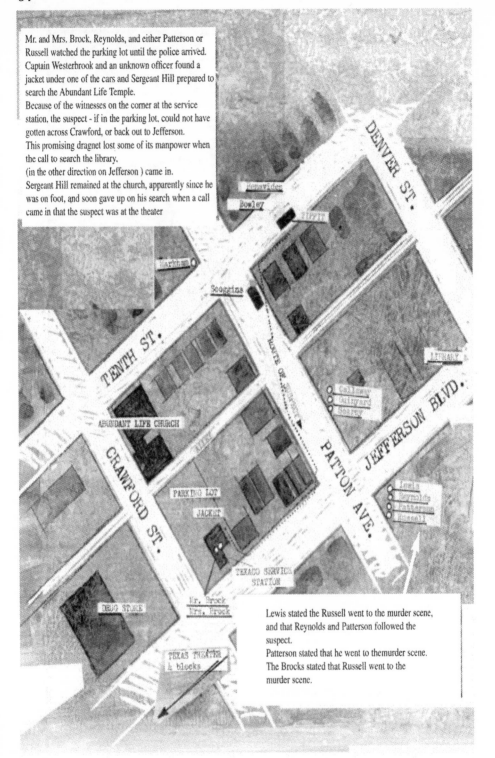

Lewis stated the Russell went to the murder scene,
and that Reynolds and Patterson followed the
suspect.

Patterson stated that he went to the murder scene.

The Brocks stated that Russell went to the
murder scene.

The Warren Commission said that two witnesses saw the shooting,
seven heard the shots and saw the man running and all identified Oswald.

The Commission displayed the jacket to six witness, only one could identify it positively
and one positively identified the wrong exhibit as the jacket that the man wore.
If the police did have a jacket in evidence,
they never asked Oswald if it was his or had him wear it in the line-ups.

An effort was made to
trace the laundry tag
found in the jacket.
Whether that effort was
succesful or not,
the Report
does not say.
The fact that no
launderer is identified
seems to exonerate
Oswald - a man who's
wife washed his
clothes.

424 dry cleaning firms in
Dallas/Fort Worth were contacted
as well as 293 in new Orleans,
according to
Commission archives documents.

It seems as if the jacket and the radio call to search the library instead of the church were convenient incidents
that led everyone to the prompt arrest of the only possible suspect in Dallas.

The jacket, the shells, and the bullets from Tippit's body are the elements of all the objective evidence in this
case. The discovery and chain of possession of each item is extremely questionable.

A study of the dictabelt recordings of the police calls made that day is bound to be inconclusive, but the details within are quite informative. Confusion and human error cannot explain the following;

When the dispatcher is told of the shooting of the police officer at 404 East Tenth, he repeats it as, "510 East Jefferson". When asked to repeat the location, the dispatcher replies, " 501 East Jefferson". The dispatcher's fixation with the 500 block of Jefferson causes him to alter the location nine times.

A suspect was chased into a church and Officer McDonald asked for help searching it at Tenth and Crawford. The dispatcher relayed this as, " Tenth and Jefferson", which incidently is where he had piled most of the manpower anyway.

Most of the dispatcher's alterations move the manhunt closer to Jefferson, the major boulevard running the five blocks from the murder scene to the theater where Oswald was apprehended. The short stretch of street was literally crawling with officers during the half hour hunt.
In the dispatcher's favor one call stands out from the pattern of clairvoyant orders; Officer Walker, specifically patrolling up and down Jefferson, reported that he didn't see anything so, inexplicably, the dispatcher sent him to the far side of the dragnet area.

At about 1:30 - five minutes after the unknown voice reported the description of the jacket - Officer Walker asked the dispatcher, "Did someone find a jacket?" the dispatcher replied, "No."

When the report first came in that an officer had been shot in Oak Cliff, the dispatcher tried to contact Officer Metzel - who was assigned that area and eating lunch at the time - but got no response. Metzel testified that he ate lunch at an establishment on Jefferson Blvd. When eventually Metzel did check back in, he was told about the shooting. Although at that time the last report had said that the suspect had passed 300 East Jefferson. the dispatcher told Metzel that he had just passed 400 East Jefferson. Metzel called back a few minutes later to say, "The suspect has just passed 400 East Jefferson". The dispatcher asked him to repeat this.

The movements of Tippit and other officers are gathered by relying on the police radio dictabelt recordings. But strong evidence, and again the chain-of-possession, indicates that they may have been tampered with. The transcripts of the recordings which the Warren Commission first used were made by the Dallas police department. Substantial deficiences of information caused the Commission to request retranscription and clarification several times.

At 12:17 Tippit radioed that he would be, "out of the car for a minute, 400 block of Bonnie View". A number of explanations have been offered for this call, including a suspected burgler and a female shoplifter who was escorted away by Officer Tippit. Nevertheless, Tippit calls in that he is, "clear", three minutes later.

An interesting timeline is that of Sergeant Hill's, compiled from his radio calls.
Sergeant Hill left the scene of the president's shooting for the Oak Cliff area and reported that he was near
the Tippit murder scene at Twelfth and Beckley at about 1:25.
He said that he had an eyewitness with him at the time and that they were driving around looking for the suspect.
In Testimony, Hill said that he returned to the Tippit murder scene after searching two houses next to the service station
on Jefferson. Officer Poe handed him the two shells when Hill returned with Poe's squad car.

Just after 1:40, on channel 2, Hill reported that:
"The shell at the scene indicates that the suspect
is armed with an automatic .38 rather than a pistol."
Earlier, Officer Summers had stated on the radio that
the suspect was armed with an automatic
"dark finish pistol in his right hand".

Officer McDonald requested help to search the church,
and the call came in to search the library, and at 1:30 on
channel 2 the dispatcher announced that the
suspect had been apprehended.

Hill testified that after he brought Poe's car back, that he had
walked up to the church and spoke to
two women who worked there.
At 1:45 on channel 2 Sergeant Hill said;
"A witness reports that he was last seen in the
Abundant Life Temple at
Tenth about the 400 block, we are fixing to go
in and shake it down."
The dispatcher asked, "Is that the one
involved with the shooting of the officer?"
Hill; "Yes."
Dispatcher; "They already have him."
Hill; "No, they said...(unintelligible)..that wasn't the right one."
Dispatcher; "Oh allright, excuse me, I didn't know it."
Shortly after this, also on channel 2, Hill asked for.
"Someone to get in the alley and behind that building at the fire escape."
The dispatcher on channel 1 reported that the man was running north on Tenth and by 1:46,
the dispatcher said that he was in the Texas Theater.
At that point, within a minute or two of his apparently ignored request for
help to search the church, Hill asks on channel 1,
"Do you have any additional information on this Oak Cliff suspect? "
The dispatcher gave him the theater information and two minutes later Hill reported that he
had the suspect from the theater apprehended and was headed downtown.

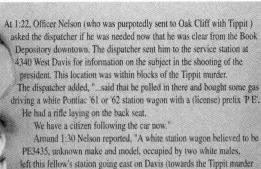

At 1:22, Officer Nelson (who was purpotedly sent to Oak Cliff with Tippit) asked the dispatcher if he was needed now that he was clear from the Book Depository downtown. The dispatcher sent him to the service station at 4340 West Davis for information on the subject in the shooting of the president. This location was within blocks of the Tippit murder.

The dispatcher added, "...said that he pulled in there and bought some gas driving a white Pontiac '61 or '62 station wagon with a (license) prefix 'P E'. He had a rifle laying on the back seat.

We have a citizen following the car now."

Around 1:30 Nelson reported, "A white station wagon believed to be PE3435, unknown make and model, occupied by two white males, left this fellow's station going east on Davis (towards the Tippit murder scene and manhunt) and believed to have a shotgun or rifle laying in the backseat."

Nelson added that he would be en route "down there on Jefferson". By this he assumes that the car turned south towards Jefferson at the end of Davis. The dispatcher said, "See if you can find that car at the scene".

The 'scene' that the dispatcher referred to must have been the Tippit murder scene. The dispatcher had already noted the similarity of the suspect descriptions in the president and Tippit's shootings, and by not putting out an APB for other officers to look for this white station wagon he allows the two manhunts to mesh into one, (or at the very least to allow the station wagon to drive off) proving a long-held theory of many researchers that there was no real search for JFK's murderer.

At 1:32 Nelson was in on the chase of the suspect-on-foot on Jefferson Blvd. At 1:34 the dispatcher gave Nelson the information on the license plate; "PE3435... (conveniently unintelligible address)...second (?) story, 1961 Falcon four-door".

Nelson's odd reply to this;
"He wasn't sure of the license number."

Immediately Sergeant Shipley asked for the prefix and color of the car again, but received no answer.

At 1:40 Nelson called in but got no answer.

At 1:43 the dispatcher asked Nelson, " Was that a Pontiac or a Falcon?"

Nelson replied, " He didn't say what kind of car it would be. He said it was a white car with a luggage rack on top. He wasn't sure of the model, talked like it was a big car though."

On his last appearance on the radio recordings, at 1:44 Nelson asked, "What was the last location anybody had on the suspect over here in Oak Cliff?"

At 2:26 a wrecker arrived at the parking lot just west of Cobb Stadium for the "suspect's car" (?) as requested by 'Special Services'. Officer L.L. Hill who came to assist asked, "Is it a 1964 Falcon?"

The dispatcher replied,
"No a red panel truck with writing on the side, license number 3E9087".

At 2:19 the dispatcher sent Officers Burton and Stanlin to 5818 Belmont to investigate a person getting out of a car with a rifle. That report and another one shortly afterwards about a man carrying a rifle on the railroad tracks at Cobb Stadium apparently check out as non-criminal since this is the last heard about any of them.

Finally at 2:33, about fourty-five minutes after the arrest of Oswald and the cessation of all other searches for suspects,the last call that is pertinent according to Dallas police transcripts is;

"Attention all squads in the Oak Cliff area : pick up for investigation of carrying a concealed weapon the occupants of a 1957 Chevrolet sedan bearing license number NA4445, last seen in the vicinity Tenth and Jefferson."

Markham and Benavides said they heard three shots, the Davis women heard two, and other witnesses heard five. The Dallas police report said that the suspect "shot the deceased once in the right temple, once in the right side of the chest, and once in the center of the stomach".

Sergeant Hill, on television the afternoon of the murder, said the subject "fired twice, both shots hit the officer in the head".

In April 1964, Captain Glen King of the Dallas police gave an address to newspaper editors and said that Tippit was shot three times; twice in the head, and once in the chest.

In Officer Levealle's report (undated), he said, "Defendant Oswald shot Tippit three times. One time each in the hand (head ?), chest and stomach".

Sergeant Owens, Tippit's supervisor, in Warren Commission testimony said that when he went to the hospital where Tippit had been taken and saw the body, he, "saw where one bullet had entered his right chest about the pocket and went through a package of cigarettes. Another one hit him about the center of the chest and hit a button, and another one, I believe, was in his right temple. I'm not sure which temple it was. I don't know if he was shot anymore".

The ambulance attendant, Eddie Kinsley, said that a bullet fell out of the ambulance at the hospital as he unloaded the body still in the button , "It didn't go into the body, it fell off".

In Dallas FBI agent James Hosty's book, "Assignment Oswald" he states that Tippit was shot in the forehead and in the temple.

Helen Markham told author Mark Lane that Tippit was shot twice in the head.

The nurse at Methodist hospital said that Tippit was shot five times and that the button and bullet clearly had penetrated.

The first bullet sent to the FBI from the evidence collection of Officer Tippit's murder included a damaged uniform button. The bullet had hit Tippit in the lower chest and drove the button into the body superficially. When Mr. Cunningham, the ballistics expert for the bureau, testified about his analysis of the bullets he said that he had to clean the 'button' bullet of blood and tissue. The FBI received the other three bullets from Dallas four months later and Cunningham testified that he did not have to clean them of blood or tissue.

The autopsy of Officer Tippit was not included in the Warren Commission's Report.

The body of Tippit had already been removed when the crime scene photographer arrived. The photo that he took showing the left front corner of the squad car and the pavement around the area where Tippit's body had fallen shows a surprisingly small stain purported to be the blood from the officer. Television footage of the scene taken when the suspect was being taken from the theater shows an officer running to his car - directly through the 'pool of blood'.

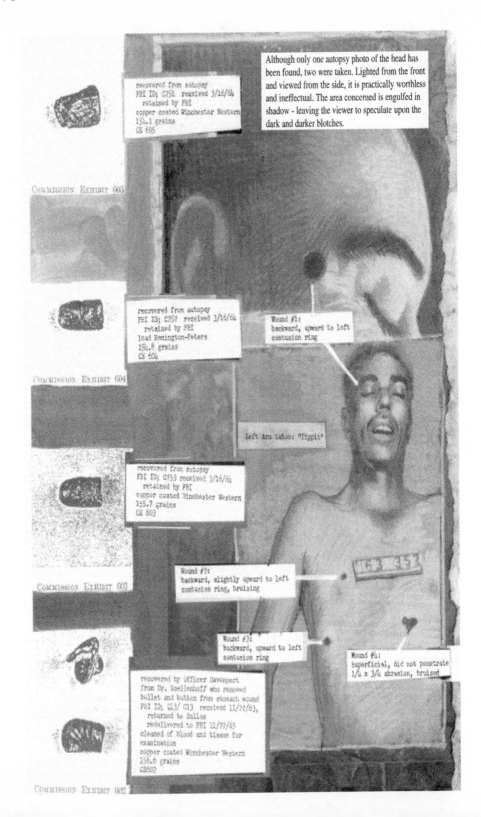

Although only one autopsy photo of the head has been found, two were taken. Lighted from the front and viewed from the side, it is practically worthless and ineffectual. The area concerned is engulfed in shadow - leaving the viewer to speculate upon the dark and darker blotches.

recovered from autopsy
FBI ID; C252 received 3/16/64
  retained by FBI
copper coated Winchester Western
154.1 grains
CE 605

COMMISSION EXHIBIT 605

recovered from autopsy
FBI ID; C252 received 2/16/64
  retained by FBI
lead Remington-Peters
154.8 grains
CE 604

COMMISSION EXHIBIT 604

Wound #1:
backward, upward to left
contusion ring

Left Arm tatoo: "Tygpit"

recovered from autopsy
FBI ID; C253 received 3/16/64
  retained by FBI
copper coated Winchester Western
155.7 grains
CE 603

COMMISSION EXHIBIT 603

Wound #2:
backward, slightly upward to left
contusion ring, bruising

Wound #3:
backward, upward to left
contusion ring

Wound #4:
superficial, did not penetrate
1/4 x 3/4 abrasion, bruised

recovered by Officer Davenport
from Dr. Moellenhoff who removed
bullet and button from stomach wound
FBI ID; C13/ C13 received 11/22/63,
  returned to Dallas
redelivered to FBI 12/??/63
cleaned of blood and tissue for
examination
copper coated Winchester Western
156.6 grains
CE552

COMMISSION EXHIBIT 602

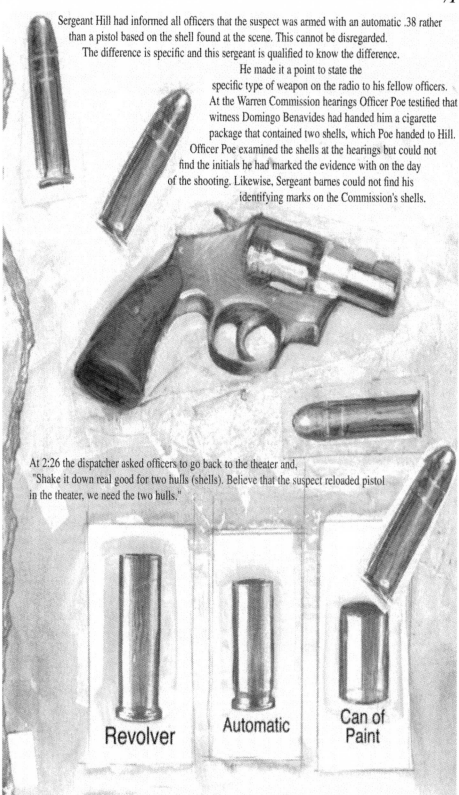

Sergeant Hill had informed all officers that the suspect was armed with an automatic .38 rather than a pistol based on the shell found at the scene. This cannot be disregarded. The difference is specific and this sergeant is qualified to know the difference. He made it a point to state the specific type of weapon on the radio to his fellow officers. At the Warren Commission hearings Officer Poe testified that witness Domingo Benavides had handed him a cigarette package that contained two shells, which Poe handed to Hill. Officer Poe examined the shells at the hearings but could not find the initials he had marked the evidence with on the day of the shooting. Likewise, Sergeant barnes could not find his identifying marks on the Commission's shells.

At 2:26 the dispatcher asked officers to go back to the theater and, "Shake it down real good for two hulls (shells). Believe that the suspect reloaded pistol in the theater, we need the two hulls."

Revolver

Automatic

Can of Paint

Missing from the evidence sent to the FBI from Dallas, which did include a pistol and a bullet from the body of Tippit, were the shells. They came about a week later. The shells evidentiary value increased when the FBI found that they could not match the recovered bullet with Oswald's gun. They had to find a match between the bullet from Tippit's body and the shells at the scene to equal Oswald, but bullets can't be matched to shells other than by manufacturer brand. The shells can be matched to one revolver to the exclusion of all other revolvers, but blast it, the shells did not match the bullets.

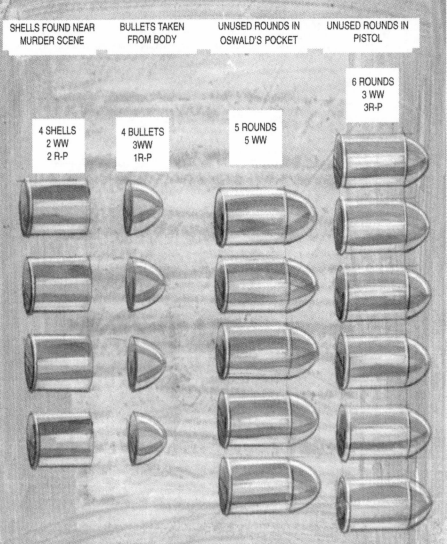

SHELLS FOUND NEAR MURDER SCENE	BULLETS TAKEN FROM BODY	UNUSED ROUNDS IN OSWALD'S POCKET	UNUSED ROUNDS IN PISTOL
4 SHELLS 2 WW 2 R-P	4 BULLETS 3WW 1R-P	5 ROUNDS 5 WW	6 ROUNDS 3 WW 3R-P

Ammunition came in boxes of fifty. No ammunition of any kind was found in Oswald's room in Dallas or his home in Irving, Texas. Presumably, Oswald must have bought at least one box of each brand, Remington-Peters and Winchester. And presuming further, he must have used up all but fifteen rounds,

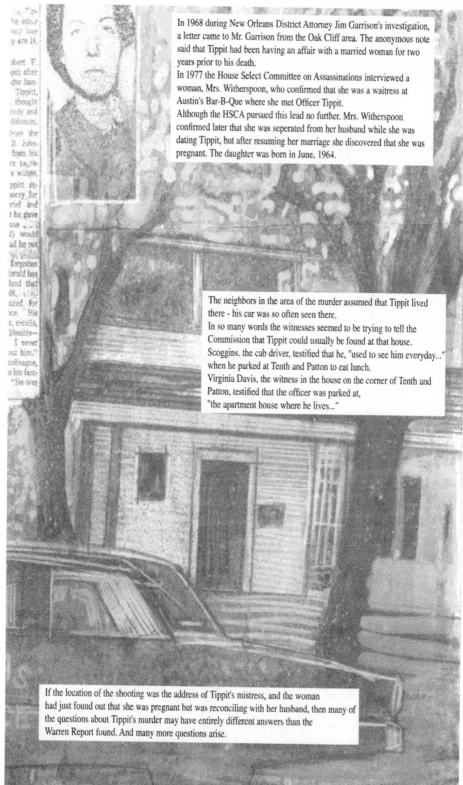

In 1968 during New Orleans District Attorney Jim Garrison's investigation, a letter came to Mr. Garrison from the Oak Cliff area. The anonymous note said that Tippit had been having an affair with a married woman for two years prior to his death.

In 1977 the House Select Committee on Assassinations interviewed a woman, Mrs. Witherspoon, who confirmed that she was a waitress at Austin's Bar-B-Que where she met Officer Tippit.

Although the HSCA pursued this lead no further, Mrs. Witherspoon confirmed later that she was seperated from her husband while she was dating Tippit, but after resuming her marriage she discovered that she was pregnant. The daughter was born in June, 1964.

The neighbors in the area of the murder assumed that Tippit lived there - his car was so often seen there.

In so many words the witnesses seemed to be trying to tell the Commission that Tippit could usually be found at that house.

Scoggins, the cab driver, testified that he, "used to see him everyday..." when he parked at Tenth and Patton to eat lunch.

Virginia Davis, the witness in the house on the corner of Tenth and Patton, testified that the officer was parked at, "the apartment house where he lives..."

If the location of the shooting was the address of Tippit's mistress, and the woman had just found out that she was pregnant but was reconciling with her husband, then many of the questions about Tippit's murder may have entirely different answers than the Warren Report found. And many more questions arise.

Five witnesses have been found since the official investigation who saw Tippit sitting in his car on Zangs Blvd. for about ten minutes at 12:45 on the day of his death. He then sped off down Lancaster.

Commonly, Tippit would often visit the Top Ten record shop at 338 West Jefferson. At 1:00 this day, he arrived and asked to use the phone. He didn't say anything and it didn't appear to the manager and another witness that he got an answer to his call. Tippit left the shop without saying anything and about ten minutes later he was dead.

One now retired Dallas police officer admits that Tippit was killed by the husband of Mrs. Witherspoon and that the police let it fall on Oswald to protect the widow and children of the deceased officer. He says that they changed the tape of radio calls, and they changed the shells.

dity as expected, there will be no need to try him in the other case," said Wade. He has prosecuted 24 murder cases in his career and obtained the death penalty 23 times. He obtained a life verdict the other time.

Questions abound;
Why was Tippit sent to Oak Cliff - at least
    three miles from his assigned district?
Why wasn't Nelson on patrol in Oak Cliff with Tippit?
How could Oswald have made it to the murder
    scene in time?
Who drove up to the boarding house and honked?
Why did the dispatcher confuse and compound the confusion
    of the location of the incident?
Why didn't anyone see Oswald before or after the incident?
Who reported the finding of the jacket?
Why was Nelson called off the pursuit of the station wagon?
Why wasn't all of the witness testimony presented?
Why didn't the HSCA consider the Witherspoon evidence as valid?
Why did the dispatcher ask to find more 'hulls'?
Why didn't anyone know that Tippit had four wounds?
Why wasn't the autopsy included in the federal investigation?
Why didn't the bullets and shells match?

What became of -
The shells marked by Poe and Barnes?
The white station?
The 1957 Chevrolet?
The suspect who ran into the church?
The automatic shells?

The questions raised by the police radio calls tapes and the suspect descriptions have no answers. Other questions that were asked had no reason to be asked. At one point in the hearings Warren commission counsel asked the Dallas Police Chief if Tppit had been involced in narcotics. The source of the evidence and the chains of possession are absolutely unreliable. The unfollowed leads and the confusion of the witnesses is more than common human error. The shells come from nowhere and lead to no one. The combination of shells and bullets infer more than one person, and the jacket leads away from Oswald.

Dallas District Attorney William Alexander admitted that once they had decided to charge Oswald with the killing of the president, his office stopped developing evidence from Tippit's murder, and ceased altogether when Oswald was killed.

Unless Oswald forgot his address and didn't recognize it as the cab passed it in, he was probably headed for the Texas Theater. Perhaps he exited the cab and walked to the theater, for there is no evidence that he wore a jacket except for his landlady's testimony that he took one.

It is apparent that Tippit was dealing with a situation other than the national emergency of that day. Perhaps the husband fired upon his wife's lover from the house that she rented, admitting the window ledge into evidence. After killing Tippit, he ran into the church down the block.

The dispatcher's radio calls also indicate that something was going on. It would be almost impossible to seperate the forged calls (added later), and the calls during the event that show special treatment for an officer in the midst of a love/life-crisis. The rearranged locations, the 'no' that the officer received about whether the jacket had been found (immediately after the report of its discovery), and the request to find more shells stand out as the most dubious.

Witness intimidation was evident - Clemmons, Smith, Reynolds, Benavides are known examples, and shells and bullets were manufactured and planted or switched.

Johnny Brewer, the shoe salesman who urged the ticket-taker at the theater to call the police about a mysterious man, had to tell the other witnesses at the theater what they were supposed to have seen.

Perhaps the entire library-search incident was added later. It was quite convenient at the time to pull everyone away from the church with thecornered murderer, maybe it was staged and taped for the dictabelt recording. There are no records of the witnesses at the library or the church.

The dictabelt's time announcements, and the Tippit /Nelson/Oak Cliff orders appear to be the most obvious examples of re-recording manipulation.

And Owens testimony to the Commission that Tippit was actually heading downtown when he was shot tends to prove that the Dallas police intended to deceive the investigators.

Dallas police altered the tape and intimidated the witnesses.
It was pressure from below. The rank and file doing what they must for a fellow brother.

The Warren Commission didn't cover it up. They actually asked a few good questions that, if pursued, might have exposed fully the Dallas-Police-Honor-cover-up. Dallas didn't want the bereaved family to face the truth, especially not the awful truth in the national spotlight. The Commission took the story as it was handed to them. Perhaps even discovering the ruse and allowing it to bolster their own 'one-man/lone-nut' cover-up about the president's assassination. All they needed from Dallas was a motive.
All we need is the truth.

 steamshovel press

THE WEB AND THE PENTAGON
Robert Sterling

During the summer of 1969, the idea of a coming Aquarius Age was floating through the air in full bloom. Neil Armstrong had walked on the moon, Jimi Hendrix blasted Woodstock with "The Star-Spangled Banner," and Charles Manson led a bloody slaughter which, at least symbolically, appeased the angry moon-goddess as she demanded sacrifice to sanctify the new era.

Perhaps it is fitting that when Labor Day weekend came that year, bringing the season to its traditional close (true, the season actually ends in late September, but most consider the Labor Day weekend the final gasp before Autumn hits), a little observed event occurred which would rock the planet in a way that - for all their impact on the collective unconsciousness - neither Neil, Jimi nor Chuck could ever hope to match.

It happened at UCLA, not too far from the sites of Helter Skelter. Arriving there was the first network switch for a little campus-to-campus information network called ARPANet. The next day, it was hooked up, and soon after the very first message was sent from the node at UCLA to a second one located at Stanford Research Institute. With this tiny step, ignored by nearly everyone who wasn't involved with the project, the Internet was born.

ARPANet was short for ARPA Network, and ARPA stood for the Advanced Research Projects Agency. ARPA funded scientific research and was formed in 1958, during the panic following the launching of the Russian space satellite Sputnik. Frightened by the prospect of the Evil Soviet Empire showing socialism was a superior economic system, the American establishment came up with the only logical response to the menacing threat: prove the claim to be false by having the government fund a huge, centralized project which was managed and controlled by the state.

ARPA was controlled by the Department of Defense, and the purpose of ARPA was to focus on leading edge goodies that had military applications. The results were quite stunning, though cynics would point out that nearly every major American scientific advancement since 1958 wasn't funded until researchers could first find a way the technology could exterminate people more efficiently.

ARPA certainly did not create the massive military-industrial komplex (Mikkies for short): this was done through World War II, Korea, and the Cold War paranoia which followed. Further, there were already many huge projects that were dubiously linked to military purposes, most notably the Federal Highway System, which was created thanks to a defense spending bill. (The supposed purpose of the highway system, people stuck in traffic jams should ironically remind themselves of, was to enable military equipment and personnel to be transported on the ground quickly.) Still, the founding of ARPA is an important event in the history of the American Mikkie, as it formed an agency to centralize and legitimize the concept of the Pentagon funding the US economic engine. In 1961, President Dwight D. Eisenhower warned the public of the threat that was being created. Having quietly played golf while he saw the death machine develop under his tenure, he boldly stated in his Farewell Address:

"Our military organization today bears little relation to that known by any of my predecessors in peacetime, or indeed by the fighting men of World War II or Korea. "

Until the latest of our world conflicts, the United States had no armaments industry. American makers of plowshares could, with time and as required, make swords as well. But now we can no longer risk emergency improvisation of national defense; we have been compelled to create a permanent armaments industry of vast proportions. Added to this, three and a half million men and women are directly engaged in the defense establishment. We annually spend on military security more than the net income of all United States corporations.

This conjunction of an immense military establishment and a large arms industry is new in the American experience. The total influence — economic, political, even spiritual — is felt in every city, every State house, every office of the Federal government. We recognize the imperative need for this development. Yet we must not fail to comprehend its grave implications. Our toil, resources and livelihood are all involved; so is the very structure of our society.

In the councils of government, we must guard against the acquisition of unwarranted influence, whether sought or unsought, by the military-industrial complex. The potential for the disastrous rise of misplaced power exists and will persist.

Since Ike bid goodbye with these words, only three presidents have even remotely dared to challenge the Mikkie establishment in any way: John Kennedy, Richard Nixon and Bill Clinton. JFK was bumped off, Tricky Dick was forced to resign in disgrace over Watergate, and Slick Willie has been effectively neutralized thanks to his Peckergate scandals.

In 1972, ARPA would change its name to DARPA, the "D" standing for Defense. This move could have been applauded as more honest, a step forward in admitting the obvious link between the DOD and ARPA: unfortunately, it has merely aided the concealment of the blatant connection. The terms "DARPA" and "ARPA" are in fact interchangeable, but appear to the uninformed as two separate agencies. When it becomes convenient to hide military ties to a project, ARPA is the preferred name in the media.

One DARPA project where there is a curtain obscuring Pentagon ties is the creation of the internet. Read an article on the subject, and the role of the DOD in the process will likely be unmentioned. ARPA (not DARPA) will probably be described as a benign institution created for altruistic and benevolent reasons, omitting that nothing would be financed by the agency that wasn't defense related.

The Mikkie involvement with the internet has hardly ended, but merely has become more subtle. The control over the vast majority of Internet domain registrations (names ending with com, .net, .org, and .edu) now rests in the hands of Scientific Applications International Corporation (SAIC) of San Diego, CA. Officially, SAIC is a private company, a multi-billion dollar defense contractor. A scanning of the names of its past and present board of directors reveals the distinction of being a "private" company to be a sham. The list includes Admiral Bobby Ray Inman (former director of the NSA, deputy director of the CIA and a strong candidate for Watergate's Deep Throat), Robert Gates (the former CIA director under George Bush), John Deutch (Bill Clinton's former CIA director), William Perry (Clinton's secretary of defense), Donald Hicks (former R&D head for the Pentagon), Donald Kerr (former head of the Los Alamos National Laboratory), Melvin Laird (defense secretary under Richard Nixon) and General Maxwell Thurman (the commander of the U.S. invasion of Panama.) Among the contracts that SAIC has received are for re-engineering the Pentagon's information systems, automating the FBI's computerized fingerprint identification system, and building a national criminal history information system. SAIC is widely rumored to be a CIA-military intelligence front: the facts suggest nothing otherwise.

Of course, the history behind the last great information revolution, the creation of the printing press, is also cryptically concealed. Johann Gutenberg, the creator, was a successful silversmith by trade. At the time, many silversmiths were also alchemists, whose goal was to transmute base metal into silver and gold. The alchemists are considered by many to be the fathers of modern chemistry, but were much more: they were occultists, whose experiments in science were to reflect their own personal attempt to purify and transmute their own souls. All this leads to some important questions: was Gutenberg an alchemist himself? If so, how does the printing press fit into all this?

Many people know what the first book Gutenberg published was: the Holy Bible. Few ask what the second book was. The answer? Good question. It appears the sole purpose of the printing press was to print the Bible and the Bible alone, and everything else was of little (if any) importance to him. Before the printing press, the Bible was a document in the hands of a select few, a corrupt priesthood centered in Rome. The printing of the Bible (and it's distribution to the masses) was a questioning of authority, an attack on the powers that be, a declaration of war.

In retrospect, it makes sense this came from Germany, as this was where much of the shattered remnants of the Knights Templar fled when their order was outlawed by the Vatican. There, they hid in the underground, forming secret societies, waiting... and plotting for revenge. By the time Gutenberg came around, they were ready, and Gutenberg, silversmith, probable alchemist, and likely Rosicrucian as well, struck the glorious first blow that shook the world. Not too long after that, another German, Martin Luther (who had a rose and a cross as his personal seal) started a protest movement that shook the world in it's own right.

Fast forward to the Cold War, and, in place of the Vatican and the Templars, there are the Evil Soviet Empire and the "Free" World led by the Uncle Sam. The Pentagon becomes obsessed with the security of their command center, namely, how to protect the war machine from destruction due to a targeted attack on the information center? After mulling over that mind bender, a brilliant answer is given: protect the command center by not having one. Rather than having information stored in one centralized location, it is suggested that it be held at multiple decentralized spots. All these spots would then be linked together by an international network. Internet for short.

And so began the second great revolution in information distribution in history. How ironic that, like the printing press before it, it was an unintended byproduct of the battle for world domination, and those who created it weren't even aware of the full implications of the project.

In 1953, the CIA began using LSD as part of MK-ULTRA, the now infamous collection of experiments and programs to test mind control on the American public. MK-ULTRA was merely the extension of twisted experiments pulled by Nazi scientists in concentration camps such as Auschwitz and Dachau, who apparently continued the experiments without blinking when smuggled into the USA courtesy of Operation Paperclip. (The "MK" is believed to stand for "Mind Kontrolle," representing the Germanic origins of the operation: going the full ten yards, however, and considering the diabolical nature of many of these tests, they could merely stand for "Mein Kampf.") LSD (Lysergic acid diethylamide, or LSD-25) was created in 1938, when Dr. Albert Hofmann formulated the first dose at Sandoz Pharmaceutic. Hofmann was experimenting with rye fungus derivatives, and in his 25th attempt (hence the "25" in the official name) came up with the master formula by accident. Absorbing the compound through his fingers, he began to trip. As Hoffman would later remember, "As I lay in a dazed condition with eyes closed, there surged up from me a succession of fantastic, rapidly changing imagery of a striking reality and depth, alternating with a vivid, kaleidoscopic display of colors." Two days later, Hoffman would administer an intentional trip. "I thought I had died. My 'ego' was suspended somewhere in space, and I saw my body lying dead on the sofa." The CIA would later switch from Sandoz to Eli Lilly as their drug supplier when Lilly cracked the secret formula, promising to supply the Company "tonnage quantities." One ton of LSD equals 2.5 billion doses.

LSD, which was suspected to be an effective mind kontrol agent, was a major component of MK-ULTRA, used in such CIA tests as "Operation Midnight Climax," where CIA-run brothels were equipped with

> **"Turn on, tune in, and drop out."**
> **– Timothy Leary**

cameras and one-way mirrors, and hookers unwittingly dosed clients to cause unsuspecting trips. More sinister was the non-consenting dosage of African-American patients at a narcotics hospital for 75 days with increasing amounts. Coincidentally (or perhaps not-so-coincidentally) one of the two sole overseas military bases where the CIA tested LSD was the Atsugi Naval Base in Japan. During these tests, a young Marine by the name of Lee Harvey Oswald was stationed there.

Among the people who flipped on acid as the decade came to a close were Jimi Hendrix and Charles Manson; considering the widespread usage of military personnel as guinea pigs, there is indeed a strong possibility that Neil Armstrong tripped as well on a few occasions.

The kingpin of LSD during the late sixties, Ronald Stark, would often brag of his connections to the CIA. The boys of Langley, predictably, are silent on Stark's claim, but an Italian judge was convinced by the evidence in 1979 that he was, and dismissed a major case against him because of this conclusion. Stark hardly is the last major drug dealer to be closely tied to the CIA (as Danilo Blandon would be revealed in Gary Webb's groundbreaking "Dark Alliance" series), but there is one linkage to Stark that is most fascinating: he certainly fits the description of a "Mr. Big" LSD dealer who was believed to be the supplier for the Manson Family. The wealthiest victims of the Tate-LaBianca slayings were likely heavily involved in the LSD market, and their deaths probably had more to do with drug debts than they did with causing a race war, despite what Vincent Bugliosi may implausibly insist.

Unsurprising, the evidence has never been properly investigated by authorities, so the answers remain an enigma. Yet the possible link between Manson and Stark raises a serious question: was the Manson Family a hit squad for hire for the ugly underbelly of CIA assets gone amuck, a gang of thugs hired to do dirty deeds dirt cheap? If so, the hit squad may have had even higher contacts than Stark: in 1974, Mansonite Squeaky Fromme failed an attempt to kill President Gerald Ford, which would've made a Rockefeller Commander-in-Chief. Michael Milan, a reputed hit man for J. Edgar Hoover, claims he was offered a contract to take out Ford before this by those high up in the establishment, and he argued the Manson Family took the contract instead.

The whole sex, drugs and rock 'n roll rebellion of the sixties has been alleged by dubious sources (Lyndon Larouche and other uptight, sexually repressed opponents of hedonistic values) to be nothing more than a British intelligence mind kontrol experiment. Certainly this is a tad simplistic, but it is true that EMI (Electrical and Mechanical Instruments), the record label that launched The Beatles, was one of Britain's largest producers of military electronics and a key member of the military intelligence establishment. Much of what later became termed "Beatlemania" was originally nothing more than staged, contrived hysteria to promote the Fab Four, a hysteria that other fans would later emulate for real after receiving the cues for proper behavior. It is further true that the LSD epidemic was basically manufactured by the CIA, which often worked very closely with British intelligence and their Anglo-Saxon establishment. Much of the policy carried out by the CIA and MI6 was first drafted by the elitist Club of Rome and their favorite think tank, the British Tavistock Institute for Human Relations.

All this leads to some interesting speculation about the actual purpose of the CIA distribution of LSD. Considering the inherently vile nature of MK-ULTRA, the conventional conspiratorial viewpoint is that it was for mass manipulation. Since the widest distribution of the psychedelic happened at the height of the anti-war and political rebellion of the sixties, it is possible the Army and CIA wanted to dose the political subversives into self-destruction. As *Naked Lunch* author William Burroughs commented about the drug (and certainly Burroughs would know), "LSD makes people less competent. You can see their motivation for turning people on."

Perhaps, and yet there does seem to be one problem with this grim, flippant explanation: for many people - if not the vast majority - the usage of LSD was extremely beneficial. The perceptions it awakened people to was of an uncomparable spiritual ecstasy, and many of the world's finest cultural works have been inspired by it since its introduction. As John Lennon said (in his last *Playboy* interview, before the CIA murdered him) about the development of LSD: "We must always remember to thank the CIAand the Army for LSD. They invented it to control people, but they gave us freedom instead." Timothy Leary boldly declared, "The LSD movement was started by the CIA. I wouldn't be here now without the foresight of the CIA Scientists." Even poet Allen S. Ginsberg asked - while on an acid trip, no less - the big question: "Am I the product of one of the CIA's experiments in mind control?"

Could the CIA and Pentagon mess up so badly in their short-sighted attempt to promote authoritarianism, kontrol and korporate profits? Could they have unintentionally advanced the spiritual development of so many people? Could they have unwittingly evolved the human species, providing us a way to better appreciate Monty Python, Pink Floyd albums and lava lamps?

Maybe. Then again, maybe not.

Maybe it wasn't by accident after all. Maybe it is at least partially true that the CIA's distribution of LSD was actually benevolent. Maybe within the intelligence community, there is a faction that actually cares about mankind, and promoted the usage of LSD to subvert the status quo.

A widely popular view within the underground information network (promoted mainly by the woman pen named as Ru Mills) is that there are two factions within the intelligence community: one that is for defending the US Constitution, the other which is for promotion of the New World Order. How the evidence is presented (and Ms. Mills is the first to admit her sources may be feeding her propaganda) leads little doubts as to which side is "the good guys" in the battle. The reality appears somewhat different: though many who fight for the Constitution do so for the decent, honorable reason of preserving worthwhile American values such as individualism, independence and liberty, there is a serious portion supposedly backing this agenda with other motives. Nationalism is an ideology which is a great promoter of warfare, and those in the Mikkie establishment have much invested in tribalism. Likewise, though there are many promoting internationalism for more cynical reasons, some do the same for quite noble purposes. What George Bush meant by "New World Order" and John Lennon meant with "Imagine" are two entirely different things, though on the surface they may look the same.

Which leads us back to Aquarius. During the sixties, there certainly was a rising belief in a coming age, an age of enlightenment where man would reach a higher state of consciousness. The belief that a new age was upon us was widespread, whether it be the Christian Second Coming, the Crowleyite Aeon of Horus, or the most popular terminology of the time, the Age of Aquarius. All these versions seemed to cling to an underlining belief of a savior or messiah, a Moonchild who would lead people to this New Age. As pop spiritualist James Redfield would later describe it in *The Celestine Prophecy:* "One individual would grasp the exact way of connecting with God's source of energy and direction and would become a lasting example that this connection is possible." The belief littered pop-culture works with sometimes cryptic reference: The Who released the rock opera Tommy, Stanley Kubrick and Arthur C. Clarke teamed up to present The Starchild in 2001, and in the most-played song in the history of Rock Music, Led Zeppelin's "Stairway to Heaven," Robert Plant sings, "And it's whispered that soon... the piper will lead us to reason." Even Roman Polanski - whose lover Sharon Tate and their unborn child were the most shocking deaths of Helter Skelter - would refer to it in his spooky film *Rosemary's Baby*, as one man's savior is another man's spawn of Satan. (Perhaps this explains why Anton LaVey's *Satanic Bible* was also released in 1969.)

To state that many of the promoters of this ideology were involved in the world of intelligence would be an understatement. Aleister Crowley worked with British

Intelligence (among other agencies), even teaming up with future James Bond creator Ian Fleming to nab Rudolph Hess. One of Crowley's most devoted followers was Jack Parsons, who in 1945-46 engaged in an occult ritual called "The Babylon Working" in the desert of California, all to open up a gateway to the new age (the movie Stargate is loosely inspired by it.) Parsons was also a brilliant Caltech rocket scientist, and JPL is called by some "Jack Parsons' Laboratory" thanks to his influence. His partner in the sorcerer rites, future Scientology founder L. Ron Hubbard, claimed (with strong evidence to back it up) that he was working for Naval Intelligence at the time. Aldous Huxley, author of the dystopian *Brave New World*, was one of the great promoters of LSD through his work The Doors of Perception (which inspired the name of Jim Morrison's band.) He also dabbled with the occult, and was involved with British intelligence as well.

This connection between the establishment and the occult is hardly new: the American rebellion of 1776 and the formation of the United States of America, after all, were led mainly by high-level Freemasons and other secret society leaders, who envisioned the formation of a New World paradise in the Western hemisphere. Then there is the fact that the symbol for the Department of Defense itself, the Pentagon, has heavy occult value.

Does all this prove there was a more benevolent motive behind the LSD craze of the sixties? No, but the smoking gun may come from LSD guru Timothy Leary. Leary (who some insist worked for the CIA as well) would claim he was asked to supply LSD to Mary Pinchot Meyer, who said she needed it for an operation she was working on for intelligence. According to Leary, Meyer claimed she was trying to change the consciousness of men with power. At the time, Meyer was a serious paramour of JFK. Soon after, Kennedy began planning to pull out of Vietnam and smash the CIA, both of which would've happened had he not been killed.

There are some who insist that Leary's story is a fantasy: if so, it has a double. An intriguing (though surprisingly uncirculated) rumor is that another female associate of Leary would, in the late eighties, travel to the USSR and guide Mikhail Gorbachev through acid trips and to a higher state. Soon after these visits, the Berlin Wall fell and the evil Soviet empire was demolished. Privately, this female associate has admitted the rumor is true, and adds she was working for American intelligence when she did this. While the acid trips may have less to do with the Soviet self-destruction than an unwise wasting of resources on bloated military budgets, if her claim is true, it would further confirm the entertaining stories spun by Leary didn't originate in his mind after all.

The idea that Meyer or Leary's gal-pal were spies on a mission certainly makes sense: as Mata Hari (or Delilah, for that matter) prove, it's long been know the best way to manipulate a man is with a very attractive woman. No less a figure in the New Age movement as Ms. Shirley MacLaine is alleged to have done this for the CIA, leaving a high-ranking Australian politician in a compromising position for purposes of blackmail. The usage of drugs is *modus operandi* as well: even the term "assassin" comes from "hashishin," or "user of hashish", as Islamic mystic Hassan-I Sabbah used the drug (and naturally, beautiful women) during his brainwashing of killers, a strategy later copied by Charles Manson.

If even some of these rumors are true, then it is apparent that there may have been some positive force behind the CIA's promotion of LSD. True, the Mikkie establishment by and large backed it for nefarious reasons, but within the agency, a cabal of spiritual occultists were supposedly bent on turning the world on into a better place, and LSD was the tool.

But was it the only one? Ironically, the one group of people who have been most skeptical about the purposes of the internet are those who have most benefited from it, namely those who feel alienated from the establishment and believe their voice isn't being heard. Among this disaffected group (who, for the first time, have been able to stay in constant contact with fellow non-conformists throughout the world), there is widespread belief that the web is an elitist plot itself. After all, what better way is there for authorities to monitor subversives and what they are thinking than letting them express their opinions out in the open? Further, the internet allows not only the ability to monitor misfits, but to confuse them and influence their beliefs through disinformation. Indeed, it is likely that many of the most successful and visible outlets of supposed "rebellious" ideas are nothing more than propaganda units, promoted and financed by the establishment they claim to be opposed to.

Maybe so, and yet perhaps there is an even deeper story hidden behind the internet. Sometimes, events have a symbolic meeting far greater in value than those involved ever quite realize. And sometimes, there are some involved with a project who know precisely what is going on. The landing on the moon, the slaughter at Helter Skelter, the Aquarian Festival at Woodstock, they all seem to be pointing to something, an event of planetary consequences, a birth of something that will revolutionize the vision of man.

The World Wide Web certainly fits the bill. For all the cynicism that the information underground wallows in, there is no doubt that the internet has done more to promote their ideas and values than those of the status quo. In his later years, while certainly not stopping his personal consumption of psychedelics, Tim Leary insisted the true mind trip was through computers, the connections obtained with people you once would never meet, much less even dream of speaking to, and the ideas that would be gleaned from such connections. Meanwhile, Silicon Valley whiz-kid turned logic-oriented spiritualist Joe Firmage - who believes he had a paranormal experience with a "remarkable being clothed in brilliant white light" - has gushed in speeches about the internet creating the first true "planetary consciousness," which is supposedly the final step before more developed worlds allow mankind into the intergalactic fraternity that was once merely dreamed of in *Star Trek.* Starchild indeed.

The World Wide Web, like the moon landing, occured in the summer of '69, a number with significant sexual connotation and implying a period of rebirth (perhaps explaining JFK's determination in having the moon landing happen by the end of the decade.) According to bible researcher Robert Barber, an obsolete Greek letter - the digamma - represented ``six'' in the ancient Greek alphabet, and was pronounced "w" in English, making the term WWW mean 666. Add up the value of all the letters in "computer" (a equaling 1, z = 26) and times this by the number of man (six), you also receive 666. W also is the 23rd letter in the alphabet, a number which long has represented death and rebirth, and a trinity of these again equals 69.

All of which begs a simple question: have all these spiritual movements that have been waiting for a single man to save the world or destroy it missed the point, that the deliverer will not be a man but one created in his image? Is the World Wide Web The Starchild that mankind has long awaited to free him from his spiritual chains? Or is it, like in the *Terminator* film series, the Beast of Armageddon, created to enslave humanity and bring it to its knees? Or perhaps, could it be both, depending on your viewpoint, a double-edged sword that is both master and servant, a tool that does to man on a macro level what LSD did on the micro level to the individual soul?

Could, in fact, the web be merely the twin companion of LSD, the final key of an occultic project created to destroy the existing order and establish a new one?

Sadly, though this theory is amusing, it is highly unlikely. After all, in order for it to be even remotely plausible, there would have to be some sort of connection between the institutions involved with the internet and LSD. Which, come to think of it, there is, as UCLA (home of MK-ULTRA superstar Louis "Jolly" West) and the Stanford Research Institute (strongly linked to Britain's Tavistock Institute and home of many CIA parapsychology experiments at the time) were both heavily involved with the LSD experiments by all accounts. Curiously, the Labor Day weekend of 1969 came exactly a perfect seven weeks after the landing on the moon on July 20.

Hmm...

Creation and Destruction, Alpha and Omega, Angel and Demon, some would argue that they are both one and the same, depending on how one looks at it. The World Wide Web is a mirror world, which represents our visions and fears. Perhaps it is like the gate that Parsons and Hubbard were trying to open in 1946. What is on the other side depends on what we bring in with us, and it is our choice whether it be paradise or inferno. Choose wisely.

Sources:

Thanks to Wes Thomas, (west@sonic.net, moderator of the MINDCON-TROL-L list and former editor of *Mondo 2000*) for the extraordinary help on this article.

DARPA Web Page http://www.arpa.mil

"Origins of the Internet" http://www.isoc.org/internet-history/brief.html

"The CEO From Cyberspace," Joel Achenbach, *Washington Post*, March 31, 1999

Conspirators'Hierarchy: The Story of the Committee of 300 Dr. John Coleman

Virtual Government Alex Constantine

"The Call to Chaos" James Shelby Downard, *Apocalypse Culture* (edited by Adam Parfrey)

"Sorcery, Sex, Assassination" James Shelby Downard, *Secret and Suppressed* (edited by Jim Keith)

1961 Farewell Address Dwight D. Eisenhower

Joe Firmage, speech before Los Angeles MUFON, April 1999

Adam Gorightly, interview with author

The Occult Conspiracy Michael Howard

Mind Control, World Control Jim Keith

Acid Dreams: The CIA, LSD, and the Sixties Rebellion Martin Lee and Bruce Shalin

The CIA and the Cult of Intelligence Victor Marchetti and John D. Marks

The Search for the "Manchurian Candidate:" The CIA and Mind Control John D. Marks

Ru Mills, various internet posts and interview with author

The Big Book of Conspiracy Doug Moench

It's a Conspiracy! The National Insecurity Council

The Satanic Roots of Rock Donald Phau

The Celestine Prophecy James Redfield

Mind Control, Oswald & JFK: Were We Controlled? Kenn Thomas and Lincoln Lawrence

Conspiracies, Coverups and Crime Jonathan Vankin

The 70 Greatest Conspiracies of All Time Jonathan Vankin and John Whalen

"The Trip: Cary Grant on acid, and other stories from the LSD Studies of Dr. Oscar Janiger" John Whalen, *L.A. Weekly* 1998

"UCLA Computer Experts Sparked Birth of Internet" Jaime Wilson-Chiru, *UCLA Daily Bruin* January 15, 1999

Robert Sterling (robalini@aol.com) is the editor of *The Konformist* (www.konformist.com), perhaps the most notorious web magazine on the planet, which is "dedicated to rebellion, konspiracy & subversion." It is also home to the Konformist Konspiracy Girl of the Month. Named one of the top ten "Princes of Paranoia" by Jonathan Vankin, he is best known for "Daddy's Little Princess: JonBenet Ramsey & the Air in Colorado," "The Jonestown Genocide," and "The Gang Bang to End All Gang Bangs." Besides *The Konformist*, his work has appeared in *Steamshovel Press*, *Parascope* and *UFO Magazine*, and he once had articles in both a born-again Christian and a biker magazine in the same month. He is currently working on a book about mysterious deaths of the 20th century. He can be bought off with money and chicks.

IS WAR A RITUAL SACRIFICE?

By Acharya S

The purpose in exploring the subjects of wars and religions is to examine carefully deep wounds within the human familial body, particularly of the last World War, a wound still very raw and representing far more than just a brief aberration in human history and in the mass human psyche. Indeed, WWII is a study of the entire human history, condensed into years and decades. It contains all paradigms, ideologies and psychoses that possess the human mind. It represents a culmination of energies that have been fomenting and festering for millennia. And it is not over. Nor will it ever be over if we do not thoroughly examine, clean and let it heal without picking at it. Unfortunately, there are too many scab-pickers who keep reopening the wound, but this compulsion is no doubt driven in part by the fact that the wound has not been cleaned properly and screams for attention.

When one studies WWII, it becomes clear that no one group is entirely exculpable and no one is wholly to blame. It also turns out that this hideous affair, in which tens of millions were tortured and slaughtered, could have easily been predicted – and thus possibly prevented – had not history been suppressed, changed and censored for the benefit of a relative few. If there is one thing we can blame in the entire psychotic episode, it is censorship, now appearing in a milder form as "political correctness," which ordinarily would prevent us from discussing these painful and gruesome subjects. Yet the tendency toward fascistic censorship is just one of the ugly aspects of the human psyche required for such an orgy of insanity and violence. The idea of a certain individual, group, nation or race being "chosen" or "superior" is another important factor. This megalomania is usually accompanied by a belief that a god or THE god of the entire cosmos is favoring this "chosen" or "superior" race, group or individual above all others, an arrogant conceit that should be evident as being false. This mental illness, however, also called religion, is profound in the human species, and is at the root of practically all wars, those of the 20th century included, despite claims by religionists that Nazism and Communism were "godless" and "atheistic," a charge also laid against early Christians for their disbelief in the typical form of the supernatural. In addition to the facts that Communism is admitted by Jewish authorities to be a Jewish creation (*Jewish Encyclopedia; The American Hebrew*, 9/10/1920, etc.), that Hitler claimed all along to be a devout Catholic and gave many favors to the Catholic Church, and that Stalin had been groomed for the Russian Orthodox priesthood, is the fact that these dictators, as well as virtually all the others of the past, believed themselves to be "chosen," "superior," or destined to rule by supernatural forces larger than themselves, which they did in fact attempt both to gain and propitiate. Be it "God" or the "Devil," it is still religion.

World War II did not happen in a vacuum. It was preceded by millennia of the same behavior on a smaller scale involving the same type of players. In particular, the history of the Germans and the Jews is oddly intertwined, beginning over 1,000 years ago in Germany. However, the conflict between these groups goes back to the time of the foundation of Judaism, i.e., the creation of the oppressive Law (7-6th centuries BCE) that Jewish, or "Zionist," leaders imposed upon their often hapless followers. Even prior to that, the area in which Judaism arose was subjected to a number of invasions and continuous battling of Semites and Japhethites ("Aryans" or Caucasians), both with each other and among themselves. However, they also intermingled, such that "the Hebrews/Israelites" were not of one race, as confirmed by "Ezekiel," who said of them, "your father is an Amorite, your mother a Hittite," i.e., Semites and Japhethites, as well as being "sons of Ham" (Canaanite/African/Cushite).

In reality, the creation of Christianity was an attempt to unify these various warring factions, while on the one hand raising up the Jews and their God as "the chosen" (". . . salvation is from the Jews" Jn. 4:22) and on the other striving to end the exploitative Law and bloody sacrifices of the priesthood, which included human sacrifice and cannibalism. Of course, Christianity also incorporated human sacrifice in its exhortations to martyrdom. Furthermore, in order to end human sacrifice, the Christians had to sacrifice millions of humans! Indeed, human sacrifice was prevalent in many societies prior to the Common Era, as well as into it as warfare, crusades, pogroms, inquisitions, etc., ad nauseam, often purported by their orchestrators to serve the purpose of "obeying," "worshipping" and/or "propitiating" "God" in some way or another.

The Cult of Human Sacrifice

In fact, a tremendous portion of the Old Testament is a chronicle of genocide, human and/or animal sacrifice and regicide or the sacrifice of the sacred king. Because of propaganda that the biblical peoples were "the chosen" and that, therefore, everything they represented was "godly," the naïve masses are not aware of the bloodiness of the Old Testament or of the gospel story serving as a recordation of a human sacrifice ritual based on the ubiquitous solar/fertility cult. Although many profess to be believers, relatively few people actually read the Bible and are thus ignorant of the blood and gore in the "Good Book," which, again, contains endless accounts of genocide, including against the Canaanites, Hittites, Moabites and others. Indeed, the "chosen" were to kill everyone they could get their hands on, save the virgin girls, whom they then raped. Other Jewish texts such as some of the original Dead Sea scrolls called for the extermination of the "Kittim," i.e., "Japhethites" or Caucasians, and the author of the Jewish apocryphon "Fourth Esdras," written after the destruction of Palestine in 135 CE, wailed that Israel had not taken its "rightful" place as ruler of "the nations" (Gentiles), which are "but spittle" to "the Lord." The Talmud, of course, is notorious for its statements against Gentiles. It is odd that the despicable biblical chronicle of horror and these other texts are overlooked, whenever the atrocities of human history are broadcast.

One of the most famous biblical stories, that of Abraham and his son Isaac concerns human/child sacrifice. It is obvious from this story that such sacrifice was common, as Abram/Abraham seems quite comfortable with the notion, and the story is written as if such behavior were implicitly understood. In addition, biblical king after king is murdered, after being anointed, just like the "king of kings," Jesus. This sacred king ritual is what is recorded in the New Testament - not as a "historical" occurrence but as an ongoing human sacrifice ritual that transpired repeatedly, around and in Palestine. In reality, the Judeans were the last in the Roman Empire to give up such practices.

The practice of human sacrifice, found worldwide, appears to have been a result of cataclysms that caused the survivors to believe that the earth, God or some other entity desired flesh and blood, such that he/she/it had caused the calamity to get his/her/its fill. The ancient practitioners thus evidently reasoned that periodic sacrifices would appease the entity/deity and prevent further cataclysm. Such human sacrifice is recorded abundantly in Frazer's Golden Bough. In Fires that Cry, Anthony Hargis discusses human sacrifice and the sacred king ritual:

"The Carthaginian priests renewed their divine power by persuading the people to sacrifice their children to Moloch. The children were laid on the hands of a calf-headed image of bronze, from which they slid into a fiery oven, while the people danced to the music of flutes and timbrels to drown out the shrieks of the burning victims.' [Frazer, p. 326. Hence, "Fires that Cry"]

"Early in our history it became the custom for the monarch to be anointed by the priesthood. A method employed by the priests to demonstrate the submissiveness of the monarch to the priesthood was to require the king, in a time of national danger, to give his own son to die as a sacrifice for his people. Thus Philo of Byblos, in his own work on the Jews, says: 'It was an ancient custom in a crisis of great danger that the ruler of a city or nation should give his beloved son to die for the whole people, as a ransom offered to the avenging demons; and the children thus offered were slain with mystic rites. So Cronus, whom the Phoenicians call Israel, being king of the land and having an only-begotten son called Ieoud (for in the Phoenician tongue Jeoud signifies 'only-begotten'), dressed him in royal robes and sacrificed him upon an altar in time of war, when the country was in great danger from the enemy.' When the Israelites besieged Moab, its king took his eldest son and gave him as a burnt offering on the wall.

"Since the penalties of magic fall most heavily on the defenseless, namely children, people who practice magic invariably adopt rites that lead to their extinction. It appears that Polynesians routinely killed more than half of their children. The same was done in some parts of East Africa into the present time. The Jagas of Angola killed all their children, so that their march would not be slowed. They maintained their numbers by taking the boys and girls of whose parents they had killed and eaten. In South American the Mbaya Indians murdered all their children except the last . . .

"The festival of Sacaea was celebrated yearly in Babylon. It lasted for five days, during which masters and servants changed places, the latter giving the orders and the masters obeying them. This applied to the office of king as well. A man condemned to death was washed and put in the king's robes, placed upon the throne and given all the king's prerogatives, including access to the king's harem. At the end of the festival the prisoner was put to death in a suitably barbaric manner. . . ."

In the Bible the "wise king Solomon" is portrayed as "whoring after" the Tyrian fire and sun god Moloch/Molech. In reality, the ancient Israelites were not monotheists but worshipped many gods, including Moloch, to whom their children were immolated. In fact, the priesthood of Moloch is that of Melchizedek ("Righteous Moloch"), a mythical character who in the Bible is given authority over not only Abraham but Jesus. Hence, the cult of Moloch is to reign supreme behind the scenes. Thus, it would not at all be surprising if clandestinely these wretched sacrifices have taken place over the centuries, somewhere in the world.

We all know very well the story of the Aztecs and their massive and bloody sacrifices. Such sacrifices were extremely similar to those of the Jews, except that we usually think of the Jews as only holding mass sacrifices of animals, when we even recognize that this bloodlust constitutes a significant portion of the Bible and Judaism.

In fact, when the Aztecs/Toltecs and their bloody behavior were discovered, they were likened to "the Jews" because of the similarities in their sacrifices. Indeed, a number of aspects of Toltec/Aztec culture, including language, are similar to that of the Jews, which has led to speculation that the Mesoamerican natives were one of the "lost tribes" of Israel. However, according to the Samaritans, who claimed themselves to be the Israelites, those tribes were never lost, the biblical story serving as Judean propaganda.

In reality, the connection between the Central American peoples, including the Maya, and the Semites evidently goes back much further than the time alleged of the "lost tribes," as the Phoenicians, for one, were likely in South and Central America possibly 1,000 years before the common era. Much earlier contact is indicated by the "fingerprints of the gods," but that is the subject of another treatise.

In actuality, like that of the Aztecs, the Jewish priesthood was feared for its sacrifices and cannibalistic ritual practices. This fear was the desired end to the frequent sacrifices of huge numbers of animals. Imagine the butchery! The priest/cohen drenched in blood, with his elbows in entrails, splattering the blood all over the "audience" or congregation, as it were. "Hey, if you don't listen to us," says the priest, "this is what we'll do to you."

While most people think of "baptism" as being either sprinkled with or immersed in water, it was also common to baptize people with the blood of a sacrificed animal or human, the former of which is overtly reflected in biblical texts. As Dujardin says in *Ancient History of the God Jesus*:

"Often in the sacrifices of expiation the blood of the victim was sprinkled upon the heads of those present, according to the rite of Exodus xxiv. 8, where 'Moses took the blood, sprinkled it on the people, and said, Behold the blood of the covenant which the Lord has made with you.'"

This endless need for the god to be propitiated by blood is also reflected in the New Testament Epistle to the Hebrews:

"Indeed, under law almost everything is purified with blood, and without the shedding of blood there is no forgiveness of sins." (Heb. 9:22)

In Hebrews is a reproduction of the sacred king sacrifice, which, again, is what the gospel story represents.

The Epistle of Barnabas, once canonical, is very similar to Hebrews and was originally Jewish. Although the text was subsequently heavily Christianized, it reflects in part the old Joshua scapegoat cult, as also found in Hebrews. The word "Jesus" in Barnabas actually refers to the Old Testament hero Joshua. In describing the passion and "sprinkling with blood," Barnabas is obviously referring to the recurring sacred king sacrifice, complete with "three boys" representing Abraham, Isaac and Jacob, to do the "sprinkling" with twigs with scarlet- or blood-colored wool tied to them.

The Old Testament reflects the constant appeasement of Yahweh with blood-atonement sacrifice. This same, barbaric concept of blood-atonement represents the very heart of Christianity, as the "scape-god" is sacrificed "for the sins of humankind." The blood of the god purifies, and the expiatory nature of Christ is evident, as is bludgeoned into the heads of millions around the clock by Christian propagandists. The New Testament line, "His blood be upon us and our children," is a stock phrase of the blood-atonement ritual and not an admission of murdering God, and Christ's mythical appearance as a "scape-god" was designed to serve as an once-for-all event that would put an end to the periodic blood-atonement sacrifices that had occurred for millennia. As "history" it is insulting and absurd, as Dujardin says, "to imagine that the crowd would demand the death of an innocent man and would wish his blood to be on their heads and those of their children."

Teutonic/Zionist Connection

Despite the fact that "the Jews" of Palestine were nearly driven to extinction during the first and second centuries CE, when the Christian tale was beginning to be formulated, in large part to preserve Judaism/Israel, their numbers recovered enough to continue the play for supremacy, ingrained in them for centuries through their writings and other mind-control techniques. And there was a significant number of Jews outside of Palestine as well, some of whom evidently continued their ancient barbaric rites. The noted historian Edward Gibbon wrote in *History of the Decline and Fall of the Roman Empire*:

"From the reign of Nero to that of Antonius Pius [80-160 CE], the Jews discovered a fierce impatience of the dominion of Rome, which repeatedly broke out in the most furious massacres and insurrections. Humanity is shocked at the recital of the horrid cruelties which they committed in the cities of Egypt, of Cyprus, and of Cyrene, where they dwelt in treacherous friendship with the unsuspecting natives. . . . In Cyrene they massacred 220,000 Greeks; in Cyprus 240,000; in Egypt, a very great multitude. Many of these victims were sawed asunder, according to a precedent in which David had given the sanction of his example. The victorious Jews devoured the flesh, licked the blood, and twisted the entrails like a girdle around their bodies." (vol. 2, chap. XVI, part I)

Later, through the conversion of an entire kingdom, that of the Khazars, Judaism continued on and, as before, was not racially determinate, since the Khazars seem to have been both Caucasians and Asiatics, who subsequently became known as the Ashkenazis or Europeans Jews. According to Genesis 10, "the Ashkenazis" were not Semites but Japhethites, or Caucasians.

In the 9th century Zionists (Jews) and Teutons (Germans) allegedly collaborated against the Catholic Church and established a strange partnership linked by their respective priesthoodsâ secret and sickening sacrificial rituals. This group was alleged over the centuries to have engaged in human/child sacrifice, an accusation, founded or unfounded, that gave many rulers in Europe the excuse to expel "the Jews" from a number of countries, including from England by Edward I in 1290, as well as from Spain by Isabella and Ferdinando. The rebuttal of those accused or expelled was that these rulers simply wished to seize Jewish assets. Nevertheless, what had been done in ancient times by both Jews and Gentiles, i.e., the sacrifice of both animals and humans by immolation and by slitting the neck and sprinkling the blood upon the congregation, was alleged to be continuing in the priesthoods of the Teutons and the Zionists. The Zionist elite, in fact, had been accused many times over the centuries of using the "common Jews" as well as "Christian children" as pawns and sacrificial victims in its quest for world domination, a quest outlined in the Old Testament, the Jewish Apocrypha and the Talmud. That the Israelite priesthood used its "own people" as sacrificial victims is admitted in the Old Testament, in which not only foreigners but "the Jews" are slaughtered by their handlers to propitiate the angry, jealous Yahweh (Ezekiel 9, et al.).

The Burnt Offering

In any case, a number of the "pogroms" against the common Jews of Europe over the centuries are alleged to have been not just mindless "anti-Semitism" by Christians bent on stealing their assets but deliberate sacrifices arranged by the elite and the ruling parties in continuation of their ancient practices. These sacrifices were purportedly called "holocausts" – shoah in the Hebrew, a word meaning "burnt offering."

In the documentary *Shoah,* a 9-hour production in which European survivors of WWII were interviewed, Polish people recalled that as Jews were being herded into trucks they were told by rabbis that this heinous activity was part of God's punishment for "the Jews" "killing his son," thus invoking the old "Christkiller" aspersion, which was used repeatedly to justify violence against the common Jewish folk and the theft of their belongings, even though "the Jews" certainly did not kill the omnipotent God as his son. In other words, they were being sacrificed to appease God. Such knowledge makes one wonder if "the Holocaust" – "burnt offering" – was viewed as yet another of these alleged sacrifices by a joint, secret priesthood and occultically inclined rulers. The fact that the slaughter was so-called, after the burnt offering of biblical priests, is indeed odd. As is the fact that Hitler received large amounts of money from transnational corporations based in America and Britain, for example - certainly WWII represents the efforts of a cabal, perhaps the Order of Melchizedek, or Righteous Molech. The alleged association of Teutons and Zionists is disturbing to many, but there are similarities between the two groups. In the first place, both are the "superior" or "chosen" race/people destined to dominate the world. In the second, Hitler himself reputedly said his ideas of genocide came from the Old Testament.

It is also purported that such sacrifices by any number of priesthoods, transcending race and creed, continue to this day in secret sites of the elite. This elite group, which includes both "Jews" and "Gentiles," allegedly will bring about the destruction of the Muslim Dome on the

Rock in Jerusalem so "the Jews" can reestablish the Temple for sacrificial rites (ostensibly of animals), an act that would certainly cause major turmoil in the Middle East if not the entire planet. There have in fact been several recent attempts to blow up the Dome, some of which at least have been funded by Jewish/Christian organizations in the U.S. The evangelical Christian movement, in actuality, appears to be funded by Christian/Jewish/Masonic money, such that American taxpayers will willingly give billions of dollars to Israel. In *Matrix III* is related the purported plot of the "Committee of 300," including:

"To continue to build up the cult of Christian Fundamentalism begun by the British East India company, which will be used to strengthen the Zionist State of Israel through identifying with the Jews through the myth of 'God's Chosen People' and by donation of substantial amounts of money to what they believe is a religious cause in the furtherance of Christianity."

In addition, as horrendous and sickening as it was, "the Holocaust" was only a small part of the atrocities committed during WWII, most of which were against non-Jews by the tens of millions. It seems that over the decades many of these other victims have been forgotten and few have received any reparations, the bulk of which have gone to "Holocaust survivors." The tens of millions of non-Jewish victims tortured and murdered during WWII, as well as their heirs and other survivors, in Europe, in China under Japanese occupation, and in Russia under the Marxists/Stalinists, are rarely mentioned.

War Itself is Human Sacrifice

These various allegations raise the question of whether or not war itself is considered a sacrificial rite by the elite, who, along with their families, frequently escape such deadly rituals. The ranks of the "old money" elite are composed of robber-barons and third-party weapons manufacturers, such that they both finance and reap the benefits of war. This "business," in fact, is how they became elite in the first place, with the first tribal chieftain invading anotherâs territories, killing the inhabitants and stealing their land.

When one studies all the worldâs entanglements, it becomes obvious that human beings must stop allowing themselves to be programmed with racist and sexist ideologies – and religions are numero uno offenders in that regard: Anti-woman is many places and eras, and anti-everyone else who is not "like us." These "unbelievers" and "infidels," in fact, are to be condescendingly pitied, hated and/or killed. Those who believe in this way are superior to those who do not, according to the pathology. And so it goes on and on without respite from the earsplitting, insane cacophony. When will humankind evolve? As American actor Gene Kelly said in the movie *Inherit the Wind*: "Darwin was wrong. Manâs still an ape. His creed's still a totem pole. When he first achieved the upright position, he took a look at the stars, and thought they were something to eat. When he couldn't reach them, he decided they were groceries belonging to a bigger creature. That's how Jehovah was born."

The moral of this neverending story is, of course, that as long as the belief in a god or gods who need to be propitiated reigns supreme, no one is safe. As it is said, those who do not learn from history are doomed to repeat it. As we listen to the ongoing blather of evangelists and the like about the Antichrist, Armageddon and the "end of the world," we must be concerned that they will actually bring it about. In other words, their delusion is dangerous not only to themselves but to all of us.

Acharya S is a classically trained archaeologist, historian, mythologist and linguist, as well as a member of the American School of Classical Studies at Athens, Greece, and the associate director of the Institute for Historical Accuracy. She is also the author of the recently released book *The Christ Conspiracy: The Greatest Story Ever Sold*. She may be contacted through her website at www.truthbeknown.com, or through email at acharya_s@yahoo.com.

THE MANSON FAMILY

Steamshovel Press

THE MANSON "FAMILY" AS IT WAS
by Kevin Belford

"We will not be used for television ratings points. We will not be presented on the same level as dysfunctional idiots and entertaining freaks. We will not debate with, or entertain, people who (in my humble and personal First Amendment opinion) should be hanged en masse, and sloppily at that. Let the entertainment/news industry conjure up and present all the phony "Manson Family members" they can find. That is not us. We are not going to participate in the media's "30th Anniversary" celebration of the murders. While it is true that we do not have sympathy for the victims of those murders, we still would not unnecessarily exploit their deaths or aggravate the justified grief of the people who do have reasons to have sympathy for them. We will let others capitalize on the dead by showing their butchered bodies on television and printing pictures of them in books.

That is not us either.

So, to answer the original question of where Manson's supporters are, I say: We are right here.

And we are in every place in this country and all around the world. Why aren't we talking to the media? Because the media is dead, and we won't waste our time talking to them. Our time is being better spent on projects where we have complete control over what's going to happen. When it happens (and believe me, it's going to happen), it's going to happen our way."
- "St. George" and Sandra Good, 1999.

From their website: www.ATWA.com

The following pages do not rehash the trouble caused by the followers of the legendary psycho, Charlie Manson, but rather provide a collection of information about those followers. Sadie, Leslie and Katie, Tex and Clem, Susan, Steve and Charles. Nicknames and the real names spill out of the books about the Family and the baffled reader often has been left with a confusion akin to having memorized ship manifests from Ellis Island. These pages, on the other hand, we have compiled the definitive Who's Who of the Manson Family. The "Family", although members say that they never referred to themselves as such, grew out of Charlie Manson's wandering around in California in 1967. No one can accurately account for all members in the roving ensemble from three decades ago, but from the press and police reports, as well as the dozens of books, it becomes apparent that the hard-core core group consisted of perhaps thirty people or so. Sandra Good who, by default, now speaks for the former group claims that the term "Manson Family" was first invented by the news media. She claims it was then used by prosecuting attorney Vincent Bugliosi to label and create a false relationship of the group. The term became part of Bugliosi's clever plan to convict Manson for conspiracy to murder and later to sell his book; "Helter Skelter".

Briefly, the story goes like this;

Charles Manson, having spent most of his life in jail, was released from

Terminal Island in March 1967, and began wandering through Haight Ashbury and other such Summer-Of-Love Californian hotspots. The 'Family' formed over the next two years until most were arrested in October 1969 for Arson and Grand Theft Auto, out in the Death Valley desert. In one month between July 27, and August 26, 1969 nine people were murdered. Seven in the Tate-LaBianca homes, plus two people connected with the "Manson Family"; Gary Hinman and Shorty Shea. Initially arrested on August 16 but released, Charles Manson was finally arrested with members of his "Family" on October 12, 1969. Also included in the death toll, on November 5, 1969, John "Zero" Haught (a member of the Family) was shot. Police ruled Zero's death a suicide. In December 1969 Manson was charged with the murders of Sharon Tate and four others, and Leno and Rosemary LaBianca. Also convicted were Susan 'Sadie' Atkins, Patricia 'Katie' Krenwinkle, Leslie Van Houten, and Charles 'Tex' Watson. Convicted in January 1971 of seven counts of first-degree murder and one count of conspiracy to commit murder, and two more first-degree murders for the deaths of Gary Hinman and Donald "Shorty" Shea, Manson has been incarcerated ever since. Bobby Beausoleil was convicted for the Hinman murder, and Bruce Davis and Steve 'Clem' Crogan were convicted in the Shea murder. Crogan has been the only former member paroled.

Mr. "Cease to Exist" was given his Cease and Desist. Manson originally got the death penalty for the Tate/LaBianca murders, and for Hinman/ Shea he was sentenced to life in prison. The death sentences were later changed to "life with the possibility of parole" when the U.S. Supreme Court temporarily abolished capital punishment.

Manson is currently being held in the maximum security section of the California State Prison in Corcoran, California, and his next parole hearing will be in April 2002.

Squeaky Fromme, guilty of nothing more than a smart-ass attitude until she shot at President Ford, is doing life. Much of what is known and what was presented to the jury was established from the testimony of a few members of the Family and the skilled work of the prosecutors, Vincent Bugliosi and Stephen Kay. Since Manson was only implicated by conjecture and hearsay, the trial had to encompass a lot of theorizing of who was in char ge and who said what to whom and when. The words "Healter Skelter" were written on the LaBianca's refrigerator, and the prosecution said that this term was used for Charlie's idea of a race war that was going to break out in the U.S. Prosecutors claimed that Charlie had heard the Beatles recording named 'Helter Skelter' and thought that the band was signaling him, it frankly, seemed a bit of a stretch. Although Sandra Good and Squeaky Fromme quote from the Beatles' song "Come and Get it" in the documentary film in 1971, and Patricia Krenwinkle used the line "coming down fast" in a letter from prison around that same time, megalomaniacal Manson probably would not consider the British pop group as worthy as his own long-winded rants to hold the title to the grand scheme. Another shaky detail of the Manson trial involved the Shea murder. Shorty Shea was a ranchhand at the Spahn ranch where the Family lived. According to prosecutors, Manson's motive to kill Shorty came from his suspicion that Shorty had caused the police raid on the ranch August 16 1969. Early informants to the prosecutors described Shorty's dismemberment and beheading. The murder supposedly had been committed in the woods and by a handful of people from the Family on Charlie's orders. Other evidence included second hand tales overheard by members of the Family about details of the slaughter by gun and knife. An otherwise credible and accurate witness named Paul Watkins, who of fered a great deal of information about the day-to-day life of the Family, told of Shorty's head rolling down a bank into a creek. Although the trial was integrated with the murder of Gary Hinman and no body of Shea's was found, prosecutors won life sentences for Manson, Bruce Davis and Steve 'Clem' Grogan for Shorty Shea's murder. Years afterwards prosecutors worried that Shea might appear somewhere and the stories of his murder would be proven as Family-folklore.

After languishing in jail, Clem Grogan finally decided to tell the location of

Shorty's remains. Authorities dug, and indeed found the body. Clem won parole. Shorty's head was intact. Three decades have past and the legend of the Family has grown as it did before the sensational murders - quite under ground. Some former Family members kept the home-fires burning and many went away. As in any large group of friends, it seems that some know how to get in touch with others and some don't ever want to see any of them again. Life proved easier for the less vocal former members and they virtually disappeared. Of the less-than-a-handful hardcore and still incarcerated ones, lifetime-dedicated adversaries exist out there. One proofreading-challenged author has kept up a constant campaign to keep tin jail those in jail and those who befriend them under surveillance. Although his basic cause seems just, his methods and the paranoia that he generates seems strikingly similar to the methods of intimidation used by Charlie and the Family members. Who do you believe? What was really behind the carnage and why? Who's right? Who's wrong? I don't know. But here is an illustrated Name index of the Family with a Who-Was-Where timeline and a Where-Are-They-Now glossary as extensive as the available information allows.

SPAHN RANCH RAID AUGUST 16, 1969

(26 SUSPECTS - ARSON)

Charlie Manson Lawrence Bailey (Little Larry); Susan (Sadie) Atkins Stephanie Schram; Lynnette (Squeaky) Fromme Simi Valley Sherri (Sherry Ann Cooper); Leslie Van Houten Brenda McCann (Nancy Pitman); Steve (Clem) Grogan Vern Plumlee; Patricia (Katy) Krenwinkle Laura Ann Sheppard; Catherine (Gypsy) Share David Hannon; Linda Baldwin (Little Pattie) Herb Townsend; Sandra Good John Friedman (12 yo); Ruth Ann Moorehouse

Susan, Katy and Leslie skip to trial

(Ouish) Laura (a runaway); Cathy Gilles;Larry Craven; Kitty Lukesinger; Barbara Hoyt

STRAIGHTSATANS MOTORCYCLE CLUB MEMBERS

Danny DeCarlo; Robert Rinehard

Gypsy and Friend

BARKER RANCH RAID OCTOBER 10, 11, 12, 1969

(24 SUSPECTS AUTO THEFT/ARSON)

Charlie Manson; Nancy Pitman/Brenda McCann; Susan Atkins; Catherine Gypsy Share; Squeaky Fromme; Ruth Ann Moorehouse; Leslie Van Houten; Randy Morglea (Hugh Rocky Todd); Patricia Krenwinkl;e Robert Ivan Lane (Soupspoon); Sandra Good; Linda Baldwin (Little Pattie); Clem Grogan; Diane Von Ahn (Mary Ann Schwarm)

BARKER RANCH RAID OCTOBER 12

Bruce Davis; Catherine Gillies; Diane (Snake) Lake; Beth Tracey/Collie Sinclair; Sherry Andrews/Claudia Leigh Smith; Sue Bartell (Country Sue); Larry Jones; Bill Vance (David Lee Hamic); Zero (John Haught); Kenneth Richard Brown/Scott Bell Davis (Zero's friend from Ohio)

(FOUND ON ROAD, ESCAPING FAMILY)

Stephanie Schram; Kitty Lutesinger

Hare Skelter outside the courthouse

AT SCENE OF ZERO'S SHOOTING NOV 5, 1969

Bruce Davis; Linda Baldwin (Little Patty); Sue Bartell (Country Sue); Catherine Gillies

(AN UNAMED WITNESS TOLD THE LA TIMES THAT MORE WERE THERE. POSSIBLY ALSO;)

Bill Vance, Claudia (Sherry Andrews)

ARRESTED IN ROBBERY OF THE WESTERN SURPLUS STORE AUG 21, 1971

Mary Brunner; Catherine (Gypsy) Share; Charles Lovett (Chuckleberry); Lawrence Bailey (Larry Jones/ Little Larry); Dennis Rice (Fatherman); Kenneth Como

SHOWN IN THE DOCUMENTARY "MANSON" (Filmed during the Manson trials in 1970)

Susan Atkins	News footage
Leslie VanHouten	News footage
Patricia Krenwinkle	News footage
Tex Watson	News footage
Charlie Manson	Interview
Clem Grogan	Interview
Bruce Davis	Interview
Squeaky Fromme	Interview
Sandra Good	Interview
Brenda/ Nancy Pitman	Interview
Mary Brunner	Interview
Sandy Good	Interview
Cathy Gypsy Share	Interview
Cathy Gillies	Photo
Ruth Ann Moorehouse	Photo
Kitty Lutesinger	Photo
Susan Bartel	Photo
Kay Wallace	Photo
Diane Lake	Photo
Barbara Hoyt	Photo
Barbara Rosenberg	Photo (unknown)
Jennifer Leghorn	Photo (unknown)

Danny, Ginny, Mary
Sandra, Cathy, Chuck
Ruth, Squeaky, Gypsy

(APPEARED, BUT SEPARATED FROM FAMILY;)

Linda Kasebian	Photo
Paul Watkins	Interview
Brooks Poston	Interview

LIFE MAGAZINE AUGUST 21, 1970

Danny Beausoleil (DeCarlo); Catherine(Gypsy) Share; Mary Brunner; Chuck Lovett; Ginny Gentry; Cathy Gillis; Squeaky Fromme; Sandra Good; Ruth Ann Moorehouse

Danny DeCarlo, Gypsy Share, Mary Brunner, Chuck Lovett, Ginny Gentry, Cathy Gillies, Squeaky Fromme, Sandra Good, Ruth Moorehouse

A handful of former Family members have been ferreted out by compulsive researchers and most usually don't want to reminiscence or apologize again. For the most part, they have moved on. Some spent years with motorcycle gangs and are now 'retired' from that nomadic life too. A few incidents from the seventies and the eighties give a hint to what happened to the 'control' Charlie supposedly had over his 'Family.'

At the end of 1973 Inyo County Sheriffs and the US Park Service monitored the activities of five Manson followers in a remote area of the Saline Valley near Death Valley California. Among them were; T J Walleman, a woman with an X on her forehead and an infant. In Guerneville, fifty miles north of San Quentin prison they rented a house.

This group included; Nancy Pitman (Brenda), Priscilla Cooper, Mary (Crystal) Alonzo, and three ex-con, tattooed, Aryan Brotherhood bikers named; Michael Lee Monfort, James Spider Craig, and William (Iceman/ Chilly Willy) Goucher. Lauren and James Willet stayed at the house and were later murdered. Lauren's body was buried in the basement. As police were hauling them out, Squeaky called for a ride so the squad car went and got her. Monfort pled guilty to murder and Pitman, Cooper and Craig got accessory to murder convictions.

In 1974 Manson (incommunicado and under the belief that the girls still followed him) gave new nicknames to his girls; Squeaky Fromme – RED; Sandra Good – BLUE; Brenda Pitman – GOLD; Susan Atkins – VIOLET; Leslie VanHouten – GREEN; Pattie Krenwinkle – YELLOW. These last three refused the titles and had already ceased communication with him.

In 1975 Manson issued threats against Cathy Gillies, Ruth Ann Moorehouse, and Mary Brunner for leaving the group

In 1987 Manson wrote to friends in Ava, Missouri that he had testicular cancer. Squeaky also had spoken via telephone with this contact and escaped from her prison cell shortly after receiving the news.

ATKINS, Susan Denise
DOB: 5-7-48

Nickname: Sadie
AKA; Glutz, Sadie Mae; King, Sharon ; Powell, Donna Kay

Arrested with members of the family. Born again 1974. Book published 1977.

Susan was 21 years olds when she took part in the Tate-LiBianca murders. In jail on an unrelated charge, Atkins bragged to her cell-

Parole Dates- Susan Atkins -W 08304	
9-16-81	#3
12-16-82	#4
12-31-85	#5
12-16-88	#6
12-20-89	#7
01-20-93	#8
06-25-96	#9 Denied 4 years.

mates about what she and the others had done.

Atkins initially struck a deal with the prosecution that spared her from the death penalty. She testified at the grand jury proceeding, which led to indictments against the others, including Manson. She later backed out of the deal and refused to testify at the trial.

Parole Dates- Susan Atkins -W 08304

9-16-81 #3

12-16-82 #4

12-31-85 #5

12-16-88 #6

12-20-89 #7

01-20-93 #8

06-25-96 #9 Denied 4 years.

The prosecution turned to Linda Kasebian and struck a deal with her for her testimony, and Atkins was convicted of one count of conspiracy to murder and seven counts of first-degree murder. She received the death penalty, but her sentence was later reduced to life.

Today, Susan Atkins is a born-again Christian. In 1977, with the help of Bob Slosser, she wrote "Child of Satan, Child of God". She runs a ministry from inside the prison were she is housed.

She married self-proclaimed millionaire Donald Laisure. On their honeymoon (they got 72 hours together), she supposedly stabbed him, leaving a 4 to 6 inch scar. They divorced and she married James Whitehouse, who has now graduated from law school. She was denied parole for only 4 years last time, rather than the maximum 5. Her next parole hearing will be in the year 2000.

BAILEY, Ed Arthur

Introduced to the Family by Bill Vance and Vern Plumlee, Ed and Diane Von Ahn were from Portland Oregon. The four rented a house in Burbank until they joined up with the Family in Death Valley.

BAILEY, Ella

AKA; Ella Beth Snider Nickname; Yeller, Yellerstone.
An early member of the Family.

BAILEY, Lawrence

M / W 5/7 125 DOB; 10-20-49/10-12-49

Tulsa,OK/ Kaiserslaughter, Germany

Nickname: Little Larr y,

AKA: Jones, Larry ; Bailey, Lawrence, Charles ; Lawrence Edward Bailey

Arrested with the Family at Spahn Ranch.

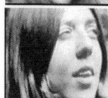

BARTELL, Susan Phyllis
DOB; 6-28-51
Nickname: Country Sue
Arrested with Family members in Barker Ranch raid.
With Zero when he died.
Sue might have been a roo-mate of Susan Atkins' in San Francisco. She was one of the girls picked up hitchiking by Dennis Wilson. She visited Susan Atkins in jail and told her of Zero's death. She faded from the Family in the mid-70's.

BEAUSOLEIL, Robert Kenneth DOB; 11-11- 46 / 11- 6- 46
Nicknames: Jase, Jasper; Bobby, Cherub, Cupid AKA: Hardey, Robert Lee; Daniels, Jason Lee
    Charged with murder of Gary Hinman. He was arrested on 8/6/69 while driving Hinman's car. He was in police custody during the Tate murders.
    Bobbie played Lucifer in Kenneth Anger's fi lm "Scorpio Rising". While in jail, Bobbie, covered with Nazi tattoos, became part of the Aryan Brotherhood.
    From his webpage;
    "Proof that prison walls cannot imprison a passionate spirit. Before his incarceration in 1969 Bobby Beausoleil was a musician who spent much of his late teens travelling the California coast between San Francisco and Los Angeles. During this period, he was on the cutting edge of emerging musical styles and played with several innovative musical ensembles. For all of the 29 years that he has been in prison, he has continued to explore new ways of expressing himself through music, as well as in the visual arts. In the mid 70s, Bobby composed and recorded a sound-

Parole - Robert Beausoleil	
B 28302	
09-16-82	#2
10-27-83	#3
12-13-84	#4
12-04-85	#5
12-02-86	#6
12-09-87	#7
12-01-88	#8 Postponed
05-02-90	#8
06-03-92	#9
04-01-94	#10 Postponed
03-16-95	#10
03-21-97	#11 Postponed
10-24-97	#11 Denied 2 years

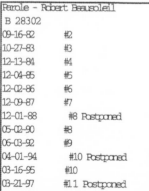

track for a Kenneth Anger film."

In prison he has worked in film and video recording. In 1982 he met and married his wife Barbara. Rumors of an Aryan Brothers prison war surrounded the mystery of the sudden silence about Beausoleil by prison authorities.

California Department of Corrections will not release transcripts of his parole hearings and they will not confirm nor deny his present custody status in the Oregon State Prison.

Again from his webpage;

"In 1993, after encountering years of frustration in the California State Prison System, Bobby requested and was granted a transfer to a prison in the northwest. The past five years have been the most productive of his life."

BROWN, Kenneth Richard
AKA; Scott Bell Davis
Zero Haught's friend from Ohio.
Danny DeCarlo told investigators that 'Scotty' and 'Zero' were two boys from Ohio who had joined the Family, but didn't fit in. They hadn't been with the family very long when Zero was murdered/committed suicide.

BRUNNER, Mary Theresa
DOB; 12-17-43 Eau Claire, WI
Nickname: Mary Och
AKA's: Manson, Mary Theresa; Moser, Lynda Lee; Euchts, Christine Marie

Mary met Charlie in the summer of 1967 after he was released from Terminal island prison. Charlie found her when he was hanging around the Berkeley campus where Mary worked in the Library. She came there after graduating from college in Eau Claire, Wisconsin.

Involved in 8/27/71 Western surplus Store robbery and shootout, Mary received 2 consecutive ten years-to-life sentences. Released on parole, moved back to her family in Wisconsin and raised her and Manson's son 'Poohbear '/'Sunstone'/'Valentine Michael.'

Michael was hunted and found by an author for a tabloid TV show. He was raised by his grandparents and has never had any contact with his father, Charlie Manson.

COMO, Kenneth
Led the Western Surplus Store robbery. Arrested, escaped 10/20/71 and was recaptured when Sandy Good crashed the getaway vehicle. He was sentenced fifteen years to life. While in prison, he joined the Aryan Brotherhood.

In 1973 Como beat Charlie up in the prison yard apparently over Charlie's request to Gypsy Share to stop 'dating' Como. He attempted another escape in 1974, and beat Charlie up again in 1975. Como married Gypsy Share in 1977 during incarceration.

COOPER, Priscilla
Arrested with Brenda/Nancy Pittman and Squeaky November 1972 in Stockton CA in possession of an auto that belonged to murder victims James and Lauren Willett. Priscilla had an X on her forehead.

COOPER, Sherry Ann F / W DOB; 8-1-49/5-19-52 TN
Nicknames: Ruthie; Sherry; Simi Valley Sherry
Arrested with family at the Spahn ranch raid. Fled Barker Ranch with Barbara Hoyt.

COTTAGE, Madaline Joan F/W DOB; 5-27-46
Nicknames: Patty; Little Patty
AKA: Baldwin, Linda Loju; Mc Coy, Shirley Amanda; Baldwin, Patricia Joan
Arrested with the family at both ranches.

COVELL, Louis Charles M / W 10-16-44 Long Beach, CA
Nickname: A-1
Arrested with family.

DAVIS, Bruce McGregor M / W 5'6 155 brn blu DOB 10-5-42 / 10-25-42 POB: Monroe, LA
Nickname: Bruce AKA: Davis,George McGregor; McMilliam, Jack Paul; McGregor, Bruce; McMillian, Bruce; McMillan, Jack Paul

Arrested with family members at Spahn Ranch. Present at Zero's death. He disappeared after being questioned regarding Zero's death. In February 1970 he was indicted for the Hinman murder and promptly disappeared again. Accompanied by Brenda McCann/Pitman, Bruce turned himself in to authorities in December 1970. He received two life sentences for the Hinman and Shea murders. He was born again 1973 and communicates via the mail with Susan Atkins.

Davis married in prison and fathered a child. An author has tried to claim that Davis was the Zodiac killer.

Parole -	Bruce M. Davis - B 41079	
	03-09-82	#3
	04-24-84	#4
	05-01-85	#5
	05-27-86	#6
	05-13-87	#7
	05-11-88	#8
	05-25-89	#9
	06-12-90	#10
	04-23-91	#11
	06-02-92	#12
	06-22-93	#13
	06-21-94	#14
	08-02-95	#15
	08-29-96	#16
	09-04-97	#17
	09-24-98	#18 Denied 1 year

DAVIS, Scotty ; see Brown, Kenneth

DE CARLO, Daniel Thomas M / W DOB; 6-20-44
Arizona/LA/Hollywood/Lennox
Nickname: Danny, DonkeyDick
AKA's: Reynolds, Danny Frederick; Romeo, Daniel; Romo, Daniel; Dennis; Smith, Richard Allen; Bell, Danny Thomas.

Arrested with the family at Spahn Ranch. Danny, a member of the outlaw biker gang "the Straight Satans". Moved to the ranch to fix Charlie's three-wheeler motorcycle, and stayed because of all the pretty girls. His information to investigators helped Bugliosi charge Manson with murder.

FLYNN, John Leo M / W DOB; 11-9-43 Panama
Nickname: Juan AKA: Flynn, John Lee

Arrested with family at Spahn Ranch. A Vietnam veteran, Juan worked as a ranchhand for Spahn.

Juan broke off from Manson and lived with Watkins, Poston and Crockett.

FROMME, Lynette Alice
F/W 5'4 115 red hzl DOB; 10-22-48 Santa Monica
Nickname: Squeaky
AKA; Fromme, Lynn Alice; Williamson, Elizabeth Alaine

Arrested with family at Spahn Ranch. In 1967, Charlie brought Lynette home to meet Mary Brunner after he had found the future 'Squeaky'crying on the street in Venice. She had been thrown out of her father 's place in Redondo Beach. Thus, they were the first two girls of Manson's gang. (From ATWA.com);

In 1975 Squeaky was convicted of attempting to assassinate then President Gerald Ford. She was sentenced to life in prison. She began her sentence at MCI - San Diego, was transferred to Federal Correctional Institution (FCI) - Pleasanton, California, then went to FCI - Alderson, West Virginia. After Alderson she served a few months in Lexington, Kentucky's max unit before being transferred to the maximum security unit at FCI - Marianna, Florida. She was at Marianna until late May, 1998 when the government transferred all the inmates there to other facilities. Red was moved to the new Administrative Unit at the Federal Medical Facility at Carswell, Texas. She is currently being held in the maximum security section there.

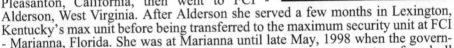

In September 4, 1975, Squeaky attempted to shoot President Ford while he was visiting Sacramento. The weapon didn't fire. 'Red', as she wanted to be called then, was sentenced to life. In 1987 Squeaky escaped for two days. She had learned from letters with friends that Charlie had cancer. It is assumed that her plan was to break out of her prison in West Virginia, walk to California and break into Charlie's prison. She was apprehended, transferred to Lexington Kentucky and fifteen months were added to her sentence.

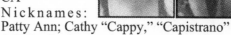

GILLIES, Catherine Irene
F/W 5''3"
115lbs brn blu
DOB; 8-1-50 /
9-23-47 POB:
Santa Cruz,
CA

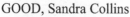

Nicknames: Patty Ann; Cathy "Cappy," "Capistrano"
AKA's: Burke, Patricia Ann; Worrell, December Elaine; Jardin, Pattie; Meyers, Cathy

Arrested with family at both ranches. Arrested with the family at both ranches, she was also with Zero when he died. Her grandmother owned Meyers Ranch. The Family camped there before moving on to Baker Ranch. It was said that Manson had sent people to kill Mrs. Meyers, but they were foiled by a flat tire. Her real name may be Cathy Meyers.

GOOD, Sandra Collins
F / W 5'3 107lbs bln blu DOB; 2-20-44; POB: San Diego/Hollywood
Nicknames: Sandy
AKA: Pugh, Sandra Collins

The daughter of a San Diego stockbroker and a former student at San Francisco State College. Although she is listed as Sandra Pugh in the earliest reports, Sandra denies ever having been married to Joel Pugh. Mr. Pugh was found dead in a hotel in England in December 1969. In 1976 Good was convicted of conspiracy to mail threatening letters and "issuing threatening communications through interstate commerce".

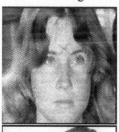

Sentenced to fifteen, she served ten years. She began her sentence at FCI - Terminal Island, California, and was later transferred to FCI - Pleasanton, and then to FCI - Alderson. She currently resides in Hanford, California,

near the prison where Manson is being held. Since she aided in an escape back in the 60's, she is prohibited from entering a State Prison again, at least as a visitor. Given the name 'Blue' by Manson, she runs a website offering information about Manson's unfair treatment by authorities. Besides occasional mischief, (she has been accused of pranks such as tampering with police vehicles) and avoiding the media, Sandra gardens and sells homemade crafts.

GROGAN, Steve Davis M / W DOB; 12-10-48/5-24-46;   POB:San Francisco 5'10" brn brn
Nicknames: Clem ; Gary
AKA: Dennis   Tufts,   Garth; Glarehouse, Clemmons; Tufts, Gary; Whitaker, Steve; Grogan, Steven; Mollan, Grant.

Arrested with family members. Convicted in the murder of Shorty Shea, Steve is the only Family member to be paroled. He was also in the car the night of the LaBianca murders. Clem was considered by the trial judge too stupid to be given death. Clem showed police where to find Shorty's body and was paroled after 14 years in 1985. He survived a stabbing in prison. He is married and is supposedly working as a house painter.

HAMIC, David Lee
AKA; Bill Joseph Vance, William Rex Cole
Arrested Barker Ranch raid. Found in nothern Missouri in 1972.

HAUGHT, John Phillip
M/W 130 brn hzl; DOB; 4-20-49 Joplin, MO/ Steubenville, Ohio
Nickname: Zero
AKA: Jesus, Christopher
Deceased

Family members claim that Zero killed himself playing Russian roulette in a house in Venice, CA. Bruce Davis, Little Patty, Cappy and Country Sue (and possibly others) were present. The police found Zero in the bedroom, but he may have been shot in the living room. Bruce Davis' fingerprints were found on the weapon. Zero was at Barker Ranch, arrested there and then released with Bruce Davis in late October 1969. By November 5, 1969 Haught was dead.

HINMAN, Gary
34 years old at death.

A music teacher who had befriended the Family and allowed them to crash at his place occasionally. Murdered 7/31, 1969. "Political Piggy" was found written on the wall in the victim's blood. Bobby Beausoleil was apprehended driving the victim's car with a knife, bloody shirt and trousers in the vehicle. Kitty Lutesinger and Susan Atkins told detectives that Beausoleil and Atkins had gone to Hinman's to get money that may or may have been owed to them and stabbed Hinman four times.

HOYT, Barbara
F / W W ashington, D.C.
AKA: Whyer, Barbara; Lipsett, Barbara Jeanne,
ROSENBERG (according to HS p. xvii)
Joined the Family around April 1969. Arrested with family at Spahn Ranch. Fled Family before Barker raid and returned to her parents. Prompted by her parents, she contacted authorities in late 1969. On September 5 1970, during the trial,

Barbara left her parents home after receiving a phone call from the Family. Whether that call was a threat or an offer to vacation, Barbara arrived at the Spahn Ranch and then went to Dennis Rice's place in north Hollywood. She and Ruth Ann Moorehouse flew to Hawaii and stayed a few days in a motel. Ruth said that she had to leave but Barbara should stay. They left the hotel together for the airport, but before boarding the plane Ouish laced Barbara's hamburger with ten hits of acid. A samaritan helped the tripping Barbara from the Honolulu street and her father came to take her back to Los Angeles where she testified for the prosecution. Bugliosi last heard that she was studying nursing when he published his book 'Helter Skelter '.

LEGHORN, Jennifer or GENTRY, Ginny Unknown

Captioned (left) as Jennifer Leghorn in the Documentary; 'Manson' 1970.

Captioned (right) as Ginny Gentry in Life Magazine 1970.

KASABIAN, Linda Louise

F / W 5'2 135lbs brn/blu DOB; 6-21-49 Nashua, New Hampshire

Became the star witness when Susan Atkins backed out of her deal with prosecutors. Linda Kasabian, was 20 years old at the time of the Tate-LaBianca murders. She testified that she did not actually take part in any of the murders, and that her role was limited to waiting in the car. In exchange for her testimony, Kasabian received complete immunity.

Kasabian's testimony at the trial was attacked by the defense as not credible because she had used LSD a large number of times. Kasabian has remained quiet since the trial.. She has married and has children and appears to lead a normal life. In 1979, she was raising four children in New England. She changed her name to Linda Christian and supposedly worked as a waitress until she was discovered and moved to Miami, FL.

KRENWINKEL, Patricia

5'6 120lbs brn/blu DOB: 12-3-47/12-7-47; POB:Los Angeles

Nickname: Katy

AKA: Smith, Cathran Patricia; Reeves, Marnie Kay; Reeves, Kay; Vance, Marina Kay; Kerwinkle, Patricia; Scott, Mary Ann

Arrested with family. Convicted for the Tate & La Bianca murders. Patricia Krenwinkle, also known as "Big Patty ," was only 20 years old when she participated in the Tate-LaBianca

murders. Supposedly, Katy was the one who jabbed a fork into Leno LaBianca's chest and carved the word "war" in his stomach. For her part in the murders she was convicted of seven counts of first-degree murder and one count of conspiracy to murder. Like the others, she received a sentence of death which was later reduced to life. Of all the defendants, Krenwinkle has been the most quiet since her conviction. Some say that she has great feelings of guilt about her part in the murders and has yet to for give herself. Like the others, her parole has continually been denied. In 1989, friends told Ed Sanders that Patricia was anti-drug and anti-Charlie. Her father has always

visited her every other week. In the early 1990's, the television show "Turning Point" interviewed Van Houten and Atkins. Krenwinkle refused to participate.

Patricia Krenwinkel –		
W 08314		
	08-11-82	#4
	09-04-85	#5
	11-07-88	#6
	11-22-89	#7
	11-05-90	#8
	12-29-93	#9
	03-19-97	#10
Denied 5 years		

Kitty see; Lutesinger

Katy see; Krenwinkle

LAKE, Diane Elizabeth
F / W 5'4 105lbs brn/hzl Minneapolis, MN
Nickname: Snake
AKA: Mak, Diane Elizabeth; Bluestein, Diane Elizabeth
Arrested with family at the Barker Ranch raid. Diane met Charlie and Family in the spiral staircase house, on Topanga Canyon road. Diane's parents were part of a commune, so the idea of joining the Family wasn't too far out of an idea. According to prose-cutor Steven Kay, Diane went to col-

lege, got straight A's, married, had children and has a house on the coast. She became a born-again Christian. Rumored to be vice-president of a bank, she was actually an assistant manager although she eventually left that job.

LANE, Robert Ivan M / W DOB; 4-10-51
Nicknames: Scotty; Soupspoon ; Bob AKA: Davis, Scott Bell
Arrested in the Barker Ranch raid.

LOVETT, Charles (pictured right)
AK A: Chuckleberry
Pictured in Life Magazine 8/21/70 with Family. Part of the gang that robbed the Western Surplus Store.

LUTESINGER, Katherine Rene (pictured left) F / W 5'3 105lbs bln /hzl DOB; 8-14-52/8-4-50
Nicknames: Kitty ; Katy AKA: Drake, Catherine Lynn
Beausoleil's girlfriend, Kitty left the family and then came back. In 1989 Ed Sanders said that she had graduated college.

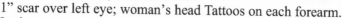

MANSON, CHARLES MILLES
M / W 5' 140 brn/brn DOB; 11-11-34 POB; Cincincinnati OH
Nicknames: Charlie; Jesus Christ aka's: Hanson, Charles Willie; Manson, Charles Miller; Milles, Charles Miller; Deer ,
Charles; Manson, Charles Willis; Maddoz, Charles; Summers, Charles Miles; Benson, Charles Miller; Hanson, Charles Willis.

1" scar over left eye; woman's head Tattoos on each forearm.

In the summer of 1967 Manson was released from Terminal Island Prison in San Pedro after serving six years. He wandered and played his guitar in streets and on campuses. At the University of California Berkeley, Charlie met and moved in with Mary Brunner. Soon Lynette Fromme joined them and the Family was begun. For the Tate/LaBianca murders he was convicted of seven counts of first-degree murder and one count of conspiracy to commit murder. He was also convicted of two more first-degree murders for the deaths of Gary Hinman and Donald "Shorty" Shea.

Manson originally got the death penalty for the Tate/LaBianca murders. For Hinman/Shea he was sentenced to life in prison. Manson's death sentence was

Charles M. Manson		
11-04-81	#3	
12-01-82	#4	
02-04-86	#5	
02-08-89	#6	
04-21-92	#7	
03-27-97	#8	Denied 5 years

later changed to "life with the possibility of parole" when the U.S. Supreme Court temporarily abolished capital punishment. In the psych-ward at Vaccaville CA until 1985, Manson was set afire by an inmate in 1984. He was then sent to San Quentin. Manson formed ATWA (Air, Trees, Water, Animals. - His campaign to protest pollution) in 1986.

MOLLAN, Grant see; Grogan, Steven

MONTGOMERY, Charles see; Watson, Tex

MOREHOUSE, Ruth Ann
5'1 brn/brn DOB; 1-6-51
POB; Toronto, Canada
Nickname: Ouish
AKA: Madison, Rachael; Susan; Morse, Rachael Susan; Heuvelhurst, Ruth Ann; Smith, Ruth Ann

A follower from the early days of the Family, Ouish is mentioned sparingly in the histories up until a remarkable incident during the trial. In September 1970, Ouish accompanied Barbara Hoyt to Hawaii where they holed up for a few days in a motel. Ouish made a phone call one morning and told Barbara that she would have to leave her in Hawaii. Before abandoning her, Ouish gave Barbara a hamburger laced with ten hits of acid. Barbara, tripping in the street, was assisted by a samaritan and returned to LA to testify against the Family.

"Ruth Ann Moorehouse, the famous Ouish and once the lover of the biker they had named Donkey Dick Dan DeCarlo was arrested in early October (1975) on a four -year -old warrant for the Honolulu dopeburger caper during the Manson trial. When she was to have been sentenced back in April 1971, she was almost nine months pregnant and she fled to avoid giving birth in jail. Her sister in Carson City helped her. Later she married a guy in Reno, had another child and was still wearing at the time of her arrest the bandages from plastic surgery to remove the hideous X on her forehead. She wanted no part of the family and had become, Mirable dictu, a stern, doting mom."

"... now middle-aged, living in the upper midwest and has three children. She was helped by her sister, and later her mother, to escape the past. She does not broadcast to the public that she is the famous Ouish. As one of her friends told me,

'She has a problem that is even more compound. She does not have an American cultural background. She didn't go to high school. Not only can't she say that she was with the Manson family, but she can't explain her background at all to anybody '. She was raised in the school of hard hippie."
- The Family, 1989
- Ed Sanders

MOOREHOUSE, Dean
Father of Ruth Ann. Turned on to LSD after meeting Charlie, he stayed at Dennis Wilson's house apparently after the Family had moved on. A former reverend of an undisclosed denomination, he also lived at the house where the Tate murders were later committed.

MOURGLEA, Randy J.
M / W DOB; 5-15-51; POB; Thomasville, NC
AKA: TODD, Hugh Rocky
> Arrested with the family in the Barker Ranch raid.

MU R R AY, Rober t Earl
M / W DOB; 8-8-45; POB; Pittsford, NY
> Unknown. Listed in Police files.

PITTMAN, Nancy Laura
F / W 100 brn/grn DOB; 1-1-51/8-8-48; POB: Springfield, Ill.
Nicknames: Brenda, Malibu Brenda; Penelope
AKA: McCann, Brenda Sue; Brindle, Brenda; Moss, Brenda; Perrell, Cydette; Miller, Penelope Rose; Tracy, Penelope R.; McKay, Brenda Marie

> Arrested with family at both the Barker and the Spahn raids. She escorted Bruce Davis when he surrendered in Los Angeles in December 1970. Rumor has it she went with Manson and Bruce Davis back to the Tate murder scene and rearranged things to give false clues, possibly moving Sharon Tate's body. Tex Watson now admits on his web site that he believes Manson went back to the Tate house after the murders.

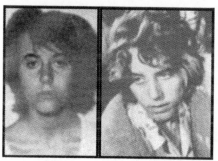

> She began a relationship with Mike Monfort who later pled guilty to the Willett murders. Brenda pled guilty to being an accessory after the fact in the October/ November 1972 murder of Lauren Willett wife of James (also slain), and served three years. Ed Sanders reported in 1989 that she was married, had three kids and lived around Napa CA.

PLUMLEE, Vernon Ray Dean
M / W DOB; 1-11-49/2-14-50 POB; Corvallis, OR
Nickname: Vern AKA: Thompson, Vern Edward; Vitasek, Arnold Edward
> Arrested with family at Spahn Ranch

POSTON, Brooks Ramsey
M / W DOB; 12-15-48 POB; Boger, TX
Spahn Ranch hand and a musician.

> Dean Moorehouse introduced Brooks to the Family at Dennis Wilson's house. Poston and Watkins moved away from the Family and into the hills with gold miner Paul Crockett. During the trial Brooks testifi ed for the prosecution.

RICE, Dennis (pictured left)
Nickname: Fatherman
   Ruth Ann took Barbara to his apartment before going to Hawaii. He was involved in the Western Surplus Store robbery.

RODENBERG or ROSENBERG, or ROGENBERG, Barbara
   Said to be an alias of Barbara Hoyt, nevertheless these pictures were captioned "Barbara Rodenberg" and "Rogenberg".

ROUGH, Johnny Kevin
   Unknown. Listed in police files.

ROWE, Stephanie Gale
5'6 120lbs brn/ hzl DOB; 3-23-50 POB; Los Angeles/Hollywood
AKA: Scott, Suzanne; Junior, Barbara
   Unknown. Listed in Police files.

SCHRAM, Stephanie Jean
5'4 115lbs brn /hzl DOB; 11-13-51/ 52 POB; Los Angeles/Anaheim
AKA: Mathews, Carol
   Arrested in Spahn Ranch raid. Fled from Family at Barker ranch with Kitty Lutesinger.

SCHWARM, Mary Ann
AKA; Von Ahn, Diane
   Arrested with Family in Barker Ranch raid. She was from Portland Oregon, introduced into the Family with Ed Bailey by Bill Vance and Vern Plumlee.

SHARE, Catherine Louise
F / W 5'5 125lbs. brn/ brn
DOB;12-10-42   POB; France
Nicknames: Cathy; Gypsy
AKA; Wright, Kathleen May; James, Catherine Ann; Manon, Minette; Shore, Diane/Louise.
   Arrested with the Family at Spahn Ranch. Catherine was playing a part in a B-movie film with Bobby Beausoleil when she joined his harem of girlfriends who were later absorbed into Charlie's growing Family.

Gypsy was in on the Barbara Hoyt hamburger poisoning; was wounded with three shots in the armed robbery and shoot out in Hawthorne, CA ; drove Shorty's car to a shopping center after his murder, and has said that the Manson family was inside the LaBianca house two weeks before the murders.

She has also said that she and Susan Atkins went to the Tate property while Terry Melcher lived there, and swam in the pool. Convicted with five others of armed robbery in a bizarre plot to hijack a 747 and obtain the release of Manson and the other Family members. Share is now hidden and protected by the Federal Witness Protection Program. Sentenced in the 8/21/71 robbery and shootout of the Western Surplus Store, she was parolled 3/3/75. She changed her name to Jessica. She married Ken Como while he was still in prison in 1977. Lived near Folsom with her 7 year old son. Indicted by a federal grand jury in 1979 for "having jumped bail while making a false statement on a loan application" released on bail, and failed to appear. Ed Sanders could not find her in 1989.It's rumored that Catherine Share was living in the southwestern US and is a born again Christian now. She is apparently in the federal witness protection program because her husband testified against former associates of his. She was living near Dallas, Texas as 'Jessica' but has supposedly moved elsewhere.

SHEA, Donald Jerome M/W 5'10 170lbs brn/brn
DOB; 9-18-33 POB; Boston, MA
Nickname: Shorty

    Spahn Ranch hand murdered by Manson Family
    Charlie thought that the Spahn raid was brought on by Shorty snitching to the police.

SHEPPARD, Laura Ann
F/W 5'8 125lbs brn/blu DOB: 4-51 POB: Detroit, MI.
Nickname: Julia AKA: Roberts, Julia
    Arrested with family at Spahn Ranch.

SINCLAIR, Colleen Ann
F/W 5'6 115lbs brn/grn DOB: 6-9-49/7-11-53 POB; Nevada
AKA; Collie, Beth, Tracy
    Arrested with family in the Barker Ranch raid.

SMITH, Claudia Leigh
F / W 5'5 120lbs brn/grn DOB: 8-11-50 POB; CA/Simi/Kansas
AKA: Sherry Andrews
    Arrested at Barker ranch raid. Tried to bail Pitman out of jail.

TODD, Hugh Rocky. see Randy Mourglea.

VON AHN, Diane; see Schwarm, Mary Ann

VAN HOUTEN, Leslie Louise
F/W 5'6 brn/brn
DOB; 8-23-49/48 POB; Iowa
Nickname; Leslie AKA: Sankston, Leslie Mary; Owens, Leslie Sue; Alexandria, Louella Maxwell; Alexander, Louise Susan
    Arrested with Manson family. Convicted of the murders of Rosemary & Leno LaBianca. The freshman class treasurer of her high school in California, in June 1968 eighteen year old Leslie met Bobby Beausoleil and wound up at the Spahn Ranch.
Leslie Van Houten, was 22 when she took part in the LaBianca murders, but was not present at the Tate residence. Van Houten was convicted of two counts of first-degree murder and one count of conspiring to commit murder. She was sentenced to death, but her sentence was later reduced to life. Leslie won a new trial

in 1977. She claims that brainwashing, LSD, and mind control by Charles Manson are what enabled her to kill. The jury was deadlocked and another trial was scheduled. Released on bail, she worked as a secretary for a lawyer. She had her third trial in 1978 and was found guilty of murder, first degree. She appealed, and it was upheld. She was sentenced to life. Leslie married Bill Cywin. He was caught in 1982 on bad check charges and for having a female prison guard's uniform in his possession. They divorced. She currently is incarcerated at the California Institute for Women. Leslie has the best possible chance for a parole date of the three convicted Manson women since her last parole was denied for only a year - usually a good sign that they are ready to be let out.

Leslie VanHouten. – W 13378		
04-22-82	#3	
05-15-85	#4	
07-11-86	#5	
07-30-87	#6	
12-21-89	#7	
12-30-91	#8	
12-29-93	#9	
04-30-96	#10	
05-28-98	#11	Denied 1 year

WALLACE, Kay (pictured left)
Unknown, although pictured and listed in the Manson Documentary in 1971.

WATKINS, Paul M / W 5'5 130lbs brn/hzl DOB; 1-25-50; POB; Oxnard, CA; Deceased.

Associated with family at Spahn

Paul became a valuable witness in the Manson trial, documenting the Helter Skelter theory of the prosecution's case. He appeared in the documentary "Manson" and wrote a book, "My Life with Charles Manson". He was mayor of Tecopa, CA. and he married a second time.

WATSON, Charles Denton
M/W 5'10 160lbs brn/blu DOB; 12/2/45 POB; Dallas, TX
Nicknames: Tex; Mad Charlie; Crazy Charlie
AKA: Watson, Charles Denton Shine, Samuel Lee

Part owner of a wigshop and dating a stewardess, mod-dressed Charles Watson met Charlie at Dennis Wilson's house.

On October 2 1969, before the heat came down, Tex ran to his home in Texas. There he was arrested and eventually extradited to California. While awaiting trial he lost fifty pounds and was unable to communicate or feed himself.

He reached an acute state of psychosis and was sent to the Atascadero State Hospital. Once his health improved he was tried, found guilty and sentenced to death. A year later the Supreme Court abolished the death penalty and Tex's mental instability improved. He found God, became a preacher, a husband and fathered several children before conjugational visits were ended. Born again in 1975. Book published in 1977. He runs a Christian organization aimed at getting Christian materials to inmates. His web site is **http://www.aboundinglove.org**. Denied parole for the maximum time of 5 years. He was moved to a higher security prison a while back.

Charles Denton Watson B- 37999
10-21-81 #3
01-13-83 #4
05-01-84 #5
05-17-85 #6
05-07-86 #7
04-02-87 #8
05-04-90 #9
01-03-93 #10 Watson, fearing he would be relocated, signed a form stating he found himself "Unsuitable" for parole.
05-11-95 #11 Denied 5 years

VANCE, Bill Joseph; see Hamic, David

WILDEBUSH Juanita (HS) WILDBUSH, Joan
F / W 5'5 150lbs bln/blu DOB; 1/21/44

   Associated with family. She was a schoolteacher on summer vacation when she gave a ride to three hitchhikers; TJ Wallerman, Tex Watson and Clem Grogan. She stayed at their destination, the Spahn Ranch. Sent with Brooks Poston to live at Barker ranch before Manson moved the family there. She eloped with Bob Berry, gold mining partner of Crockett's.

Although a part of the Family at one time, for one reason or another, the last two names are hardly ever considered to be 'true' followers of Manson, but they were tangentially involved with Charlie and Family.

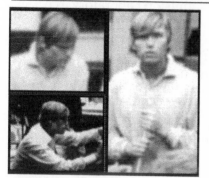

MELCHER, Terry
Son of actress Doris Day.
   Terry was a music producer and introduced to Manson by Dennis Wilson of The Beach Boys. He was invited out to the ranch a number of times to hear Charlie and the Family perform, but he never considered any recording possibilities for the music. Terry lived at the house where Tate murders occurred and apparently that is how Manson and the gang knew of the residence, although they also knew that Terry had moved from there.

WILSON, Dennis Carl M / W 5'10 150lbs brn/blu DOB; 12-4-44/ 43
Deceased 12/27/83 - Drowned, Marina DelRey.
   Member of The Beachboys recording group Associated with Manson.
   Dennis picked up two young females hitchhiking one day named Ella Snider and Patricia Krenwinkle. He brought them back to his house and they invited the rest of the Family.
   Charlie planned to launch his stellar career as a folk singer with the help of his friend Dennis Wilson of the Beach Boys. Before moving to the Spahn Ranch Charlie was a permanent fixture at Dennis' Malibu home. When too many freaky people started showing up, Dennis asked Charlie to leave. Nonetheless, they remained good friends. Dennis thought Charlie was very talented and bought one of his songs, "Cease to Exist". The Beach Boys released it as "Never Learn Not to Love" on their album "20/20."

JOHN WHITESIDE PARSONS:
ANTI-CHRIST SUPERSTAR
by Richard Metzger

"All stories are true, every last one of them. All myths, all legends, all fables. If you believe them true, then they are true. If you don't believe them, then all that can be said is that they are true for someone else." -Dave Sim, *Cerebus*.

When the history of the American space program is finally written, no figure will stand out quite like John Whiteside Parsons. Remarkably handsome, dashing and brilliant, "Jack" Parsons was one of the founders of the experimental rocket research group at Cal Tech and the group's seven acre Arroyo Seco testing facility would eventually become Jet Propulsion Laboratory, NASA's rocket design center.

Werner von Braun claimed it was the self-taught Parsons, not himself, who was the true father of the American space program for his contribution to the development of solid rocket fuel. Although Parsons has been memorialized with a statue at JPL and has had a crater on the dark side of the moon named in his honor, his story remains shrouded in mystery —for what is little known about this legend of aerospace engineering is that Parsons was an avid practitioner of the occult sciences, and for several years, Aleister Crowley's hand-picked leader of the US branch of the Ordo Templi Orientis, the Southern California-based Agape Lodge.

Parsons was born in Los Angeles on October 2, 1914, the son of a wealthy and well connected family living in a sprawling mansion on Pasadena's "Millionaire Row." His father worked for Woodrow Wilson. After his parents divorce, the solitary childhood of Parsons imbued him with a deep hatred of authority, and a contempt for any sort of interference in his activity. Parsons interest in the occult apparently commenced at an early age and in one of his diaries he claimed to have visibly evoked Satan at the tender age of 13.

After discovering Crowley's philosophy of Thelema (Greek for 'true will'), Parsons joined the Agape« Lodge in 1941. Wilfred T. Smith, the expatriate Englishman who started the order in the early 1930's with a charter from the Great Beast himself, wrote of Parsons in a letter to Crowley: "I think I have at long last a really excellent man, John Parsons. And starting next Tuesday he begins a course of talks with a view to enlarging our scope. He has an excellent mind and much better intellect than myself... John Parsons is going to be valuable."

Another member of the Lodge, Crowley's old friend, actress Jane Wolfe described Parsons as "26 years of age, 6'2", vital, potentially bisexual at the very least, University of the State of California and Cal Tech, now engaged in Cal Tech chemical laboratories developing 'bigger and better' explosives for Uncle Sam. Travels under sealed orders from the government. Writes poetry — 'sensuous only', he says. Lover of music, which he seems to know thoroughly. I see him as the real successor of

Therion [Crowley]. Passionate; and has made the vilest analyses result in a species of exaltation after the event. Has had mystical experiences which gave him a sense of equality all round, although he is hierarchical in feeling and in the established order."

Parsons rose quickly through the ranks, taking over the Agape Lodge from Smith at Crowley's decree within a year.

"For I am BABALON, and she my daughter, unique
and there shall be no other women like her.
-The Book of Babalon, verse 37

In one of the most celebrated feats in magickal history, Parsons and pre-Dianetics L. Ron Hubbard (whose role is too complicated to describe in this short essay) performed "The Babalon Working," a daring attempt to shatter the boundaries of time and space and intended to bring about, in Parsons own words, "love, understanding, and Dionysian freedom [...] the necessary counterbalance or correspondence to the manifestation of Horus."

The above reference recalls Crowley's announcement of the Aeon of Horus, described in his *Book of the Law* (*Liber AL vel Legis*), a blasphemous, strangely beautiful, prose poem which Crowley 'received' from a discarnate entity called Aiwass in Cairo in 1904. Crowley, self-styled "Great Beast 666," considered himself the avatar of the Antichrist and the *Book of the Law* is a proclamation that the era of the "slave gods" (Osiris, Mohammed, Jesus) had come to an end and that the Age of Horus and "the Crowned and Conquering Child" had begun. In its infancy, Crowley predicted, the Aeon would be characterized by the magickal formula of bloodshed and blind force, the tearing down of the established orders to make way for the new. Crowley held the two World Wars as evidence of this, but did not see the Horus-force, as evil, rather as embodying the innocence of a hyperactive child who is like a bull in a china shop. Babalon, a Thelemic counterpart of Kali or Isis, was described by Parsons as, "... black, murderous and horrible, but Her hand is uplifted in blessing and reassurance: the reconciliation of opposites, the apotheosis of the impossible."

The impossible was precisely what Jack Parsons, the scientific sorcerer, had in mind.

Lucifer Rising...

In its initial stages, The Babalon Working was intended to attract an "elemental" to serve as a partner for Parsons' elaborate sex magick rituals. The method employed was that of the solo "VIII Degree" working of the O.T.O, the quasi-Masonic organization reformulated by Crowley in the earlier part of the century in accordance with his "Do What Thou Wilt" mythos of Thelema. Parsons used his 'magickal wand' to whip up a vortex of energy so the elemental would be summoned. Translated into plain English, Parsons jerked off in the name of spiritual advancement whilst Hubbard (referred to as "The Scribe" in the diary of the event) scanned the astral plane for signs and visions.

Apparently, it worked. In a letter to Crowley dated February 23, 1946, Parsons exclaimed "I have my elemental! She turned up one night after the conclusion of the Operation, and has been with me since."

The elemental was a green-eyed, flaming redhead named Marjorie Cameron, (later of Kenneth Anger's *Inauguration of the Pleasure Dome* film, an artist of some reknown and a primary force in the New Age "Goddess" movement). Cameron was only too happy to participate in Parson's sex magick and now Parsons could get down to the real business of the Babalon Working: the birthing of a "moonchild" or homunculus. The operation was formulated to open an interdimensional doorway, rolling out the red carpet for the appearance of the goddess Babalon in human form, employing the Enochian Calls [angelic language] of Elizabethan magus John Dee and the attraction of the sex force of the duo's copulation to this end.

As Paul Rydeen points out in his extended essay *Jack Parsons and the Fall of Babalon*: "The purpose of Parson's operation has been underemphasized. He sought to produce a magickal child who would be a product of her environment rather than of her heredity. Crowley himself describes the Moonchild in just these terms. The Babalon Working itself was preparation for what was to come: a Thelemic messiah." To wit: Babalon incarnate as a *living* female, the Scarlet Woman as consort to the Antichrist, bride of the Beast 666. In effect, Parsons also claimed the mantle of Antichrist for himself, as the magickal heir of Crowley prophesied in *Liber AL*: "The child of thy bowels, he shall behold them [the mysteries of the Apocalypse]. Expect him not from the East, nor from the West, for from no expected house cometh that child."

Without the Scarlet Woman, the Antichrist cannot make his manifestation, the eschatological formula must first be complete. In whiter words, with the magickal rites of the Babalon Working, it was Parson's goal to bring on the Apocalypse.

James Dean of the Occult

Parsons' Babalon gambit was dazzling to say the least: If the earth must first be covered in evil before the return of the Christ consciousness and the final triumph of good, what better way to hasten the uplifting of humanity than to rip an alchemical hole in the fabric of reality and invite the very spawn of Hell in for a rip-snorting orgy of howling madness?

So much is written of Parsons as a psychotic lunatic, but I put it to you dear reader, is the Babalon Working the product of a deranged mind or the ultimate exploration of the absolute *furthest* reaches of consciousness, putting the peddle to the metal for the living end in revolutionary chic and mind expansion?

Parson's perverse 'imitation of Christ' was intended to disrupt, oppose, and subvert the established order of things. It's the age old Manichaean battle between good and evil, the forces of order and chaos, the status quo versus revolutionary tendencies. But in the 20th century, these lines have become significantly blurred: If you consider the New World Order multinational corporate monoliths poisoning the planet and reducing mankind to the level of wage slavery for the benefit of the very few to be representative of the 'good,' then the Babalon Working must sound like the most outright evil deed ever perpetrated by a human being. But if you're like me, and would dearly love to see the vile, puss-ridden edifice of Western society burned to the ground, you should see Parsons as the penultimate style icon of psycho-sexual/magickal insurrection, a truly American original if ever there was one. This darkly handsome, genius scientist, was, I submit, the James Dean of the Occult — one spectacularly cool motherfucker.

"Only in the irrational and unknown direction can we come to it [wisdom] again" -Jack Parsons in a letter to Marjorie Cameron, late 1940s.

The question must be asked: Who is the greater hero — he who prolongs the agony of this pathetic existence or he who opens wide the Pandora's Box of perdition knowing that this is how the final eschatological chapter must play itself out?

Isn't the Great Work, the cosmic perfection of mankind, the final goal of the alchemists? Just as the rocket scientist Parsons was willing to play dice with heavy explosives, Parsons, the nuclear age warlock was willing to play with fire of a very different sort. Parsons rests firmly in the tradition of the fraternity of Western Magi who include Moses, Solomon, Jesus Christ, John Dee, Adam Weishaupt, Crowley, Gurdjieff and

Timothy Leary — great revolutionaries and liberators all.

Parsons wrote in his *Manifesto of the Anti-Christ*: "An end to the pretence (sic), and lying hypocrisy of Christianity. An end to the servile virtues, and superstitious restrictions. An end to the slave morality. An end to prudery and shame, to guild and sin, for these are of the only evil the sun, that is fear. An end to all authority that is not based on courage and manhood, to the authority of lying priests, conniving judges, blackmailing police, and an end to the servile flattery and cajolery of mods, the coronations of mediocraties, the ascension of dolts."

Amen to that! Parsons was clearly willing to put his money where his mouth was! Abbie Hoffman, Subcomandante Insurgente Marcos and Che Guevara seem total *pussies* in comparison.

Forget your Conspiracy Theory 101, the Illuminati are *not* the bad guys and George Bush was never a member and neither is Henry Kissinger. If, in the words of Christ, it is by their fruits and works that men shall be judged, would *you* want the Mai Lai massacre or the Gulf War slaughter staining *your* karma?

Hey, being the Antichrist is a dirty job, but *somebody* has to do it.

It's not such a black and white world anymore.

A Magickal Call to Arms

"Parsons opened a door and something flew in." -Kenneth Grant, *Outside the Circles of Time.*

Did the Babalon Working actually *work*? For the sake of argument, if you believe it to be true, it's true *enough*. As a metaphor or a myth to explain the psychic and atmospheric turbulence taking place in the world today, it certainly works for me. What has long been prophesied by the world's major spiritual traditions is now coming to pass. Turn on CNN for a couple of hours for *ample* proof: wars, killer viruses, floods, famines, violent crime, earthquakes, Armageddon cults armed with nerve gas, suicide bombers; Heaven's Gate; the list goes on and on. Certainly Parsons untimely death in a 1952 chemical explosion would leave the crown of the "conquering child" unclaimed to this day as Thelemites continue to await their Chaos Messiah, but perhaps Parsons was *an* Antichrist and his particular mission was to crack open the Apocalyptic gateway and activate the occult forces necessary for the upheaval of consciousness.

The apostles of the new forms of gnosis unearthed by the Babalon Working will be art, the inspired initiator of sacred science and the torch of Gods appearing in new and unexpected forms in the unfolding of the divine drama. The poets, artists, philosophers and thinkers will form the first ranks of perfected humanity and no rules will apply save for freedom and nobility beyond the Kali Yuga.

But this will not happen without a struggle between the forces of control, black magick, and oppressive boredom on one hand and the Luciferian agents of wisdom, unleashed creativity and anarchic rebellion on the other. What we have been brainwashed to believe is "good": patriotism, so-called "free" enterprise, private property, Christianity (not the teachings of Christ, but the hateful travesty that the religion bearing his name has become thanks to the likes of Pat Robertson and his filthy ilk), is now beginning to be seen by the emerging generation of the crowned and conquering child to be the deathtrip bullshit it truly is.

A whole culture is collapsing and a new one is about to be born. Jack Parsons would be pleased.

Richard Metzger is the editor of *DisInformation* (http://www.dis-info.com) and would like to gratefully acknowledge the valuable conversations with Grant Morrison and the enigmatic being known only as Brother Blue (http://www.brotherblue.org) that helped in preparation of this essay.

STEAMSHOVEL PRESS

REMOTE VIEWING AND MIND CONTROL: CO-OPTING THE "INNER-NET"
By Greg Bishop

Greg Bishops edits and published *The Excluded Middle.* exclmid@primenet.com

There is an internet that has no server fees, no expensive hardware hookups, no phone lines. And like the Internet that began as a DARPA project in 1969, it has been co-opted by the military-industrial establishment for its unlimited potential. Information on this system can be looked up, retrieved, sent, and posted. There are viruses here too. The device that logs onto this etheric information superhighway is the human biocomputer, and what we shall refer to as the "Innernet" is the oldest form of telecommunication known: the realm of psychic functioning. Military personnel been able to "remote view" distant places and targets, and some may be able to use the power of their intentions to disorient, cause disease, and perhaps even kill. And like some kind of psychic Java script, some talented people may have also successfully bypassed normal channels of electromagentic communication to operate computers and machinery from distant locations by thought control. Although former members of the DOD's remote viewing project insist that their task was only to gather intelligence data, other information sources suggest that other agencies may have delved into remote influence of the human mind, as well as physical and psychological harm. With a few facts clutched firmly in hand, let's indulge in some history, some revelation, some realization, and a little extrapolation.

Is This Stuff For Real?

A recent documentary on the Discovery channel showed that domesticated dogs will jump up and run to the window to look for their owners the moment that they think of returning home from a distant location. How do they know to do this? Parasychological researchers have been studying telepathy and precognition for over 100 years, and have come to the conclusion that not only space, but time is not an obstacle to the human mind, given the proper conditions. Perception at a distance is nothing new in the field of parapsychology. In the 1920s, a French scientist, Ren_ Warcolier, conducted transatlantic sensing experiments. The American socialist novelist Upton Sinclair took time out from running for governor of California and uncovering the abuses of the meatpacking industry to conduct informal psychical research which he pursued over a period of years with his wife Mary. He described these experiences in a 1930 book, *Mental Radio.* Sinclair would draw a picture in one room of their Long Beach, California home and call out that he was ready. Concentrating for a few moments, his wife then produced drawings that were amazingly similar, or even identical to his. Mary Sinclair tried these experiments with her brother, who lived 40 miles away in Pasadena, with similar, sometimes superior results, anticipating what would later be dubbed "remote viewing."

The Public Affairs Office of the Central Intelligence Agency announced on September 6, 1995 that it had been involved in "psychic spying" for the better part of 18 years. Since then, the term "remote viewing" has become one of the hottest buzzwords on the UFO/ paranormal/ Art Bell circuit. Former members of what became an Army/ Department Of Defense joint project under a variety of code names have since come forward with their stories, and begun to teach this talent to civilians for hefty fees. "R.V." has become the spoon-bending of the late 1990s. The shorthand designation for parapsychological functioning is designated by the Greek letter psi (y) and is making its way into common parlance.

Beginning in 1971, Ingo Swann, a New York artist and psychic of some note, became involved in experiments with three doctorate-level scientists from the American Society for Psychical Research in which he located hidden objects by mental concentration. After some success in these trials, Swann coined the term "remote viewing" to describe his method, although he still maintains that the phrase "remote sensing" portrays his process more accurately. As the tests became more sophisticated, the research team moved the targeted objects outside of the building, and then to more distant locations. For these experiments, one researcher would stay in an area for a prearranged period to act as a "beacon" for Swann. This method was adopted in experiments in the latter 1970s, when the associate who left the lab setting was called an "outbounder." Swann claims he was courted by CIA agents even at this early date, asking him how he might defend against Soviet threats in the parapsychological realm, and help to close the "psychic gap."

The infamous Sid Gottlieb, chief officer of the Technical Services Division of the CIA in the early 1960s, had delved into the realm of parapsychology when he commissioned a study of its possible applications for intelligence gathering and remote influence of human minds under the banner of the notorious project MKULTRA. Steven Abrams, of the Parapsychological Lab at Oxford University, England was contracted to assess the possibilities, but he concluded that not enough was known about the phenomenon at the time to harness it for practical use. Gottlieb went back to slipping LSD to unsuspecting subjects, and hiring hookers to dope up men and find out if marijuana would make them more loose-lipped.

A Short History of the D.O.D.'s Remote Viewing Program

Through a mutual friend, Cleve Backster, Swann contacted Dr. Hal Puthoff of Stanford Research Institute in Palo Alto, California. Formerly an intelligence officer in the U.S. Navy, he had later also worked for the National Security Agency. Puthoff was studying lasers, but was also interested in how physical theory could possibly encompass all life processes, and presumably consciousness as well.

In June of 1972, Swann came out to the west coast to meet with the budding parasychologist and demonstrate his abilities. On the campus of Stanford University, while under the scrutiny of two other scientists (and Puthoff) Swann was able to repeatedly disturb a shielded magnetometer. He also sketched a diagram of the concealed device. This ability to affect the inner workings of delicate scientific devices, as well as the remote perception of design details, was one of the main reasons that the military became interested in psychic research. Another was the fact that over time, aviators and their support crews had noticed that sensitive instruments in fighter jets would work quite normally during simulations, but occasionally seemed to malfunction at just the wrong time (in the midst of a dogfight, for example.) One of the few x-factors considered was that the pilot's emotional state may have been the culprit.

Puthoff wrote a paper about his experience with Swann, and its implications. Government support for psychic research had always been dubious at best, and intelligence services, particularly the CIA, were looking for private sources of information. Within weeks after his paper was released, two agents showed up at SRI, very interested in Puthoff's findings and willing to petition the big boys for funding if he would conduct a specific series of experiments with Swann. These tests were also successful, and by Puthoff's own admission, he was granted about $50,000 in US tax dollars to study Swann, his capabilities, and further methods of remote sensing. At this point one of Puthoff's colleagues, plasma physicist and an old hand at para-psychology, Russell Targ, joined the team. Called the "Biofields Measurement Program," the project ran for eight months, from January to August, 1973. Puthoff, Targ, and Swann began to wonder if a "beacon" was even necessary. Computer scientist and UFO researcher Jacques Vall_e suggested to his friend Puthoff that they simply use an address as a targeting method. This was the birth of Coordinate Remote Viewing, or CRV.

The three researchers were also all former members of Scientology, and although some authors insist that the project was riddled with the influence of Dianetics, there appears to be little evidence for this. They had let their memberships lapse years before, and reveal none of the Scientologist dogma in their writings.

Towards the end of these experiments, Puthoff received a phone call from a former entrepreneur and later Police Commissioner of Burbank, California, Pat Price. Price told Puthoff that he had used his extranormal abilities to solve baffling crimes, but had considered his strange talent just run-of-the-mill intuition until he began night-ly "travels" to political and military hot spots around the globe, gathering information that was confirmed later by news reports. He "began to wonder if all this psychic stuff I had put down for years might have something to it." On an impulse, Puthoff read him off a series of CRV coordinates given to him by his CIA contacts. Three days later, a letter from Price described the geographical target from a height of 1500 feet, and proceeded on a "tour" of the building, moving down hallways, entering rooms, and later, for good measure, reading names off desks, and the labels on files in a locked cabinet. The facility was a magnetically shielded, underground NSA installation in Virginia. The shocked CIA personnel were investigated for a possible breach of security. Price later calmed things down by remote viewing a similar site in the Soviet Union without coordinates or prompting. For the CIA, this established that RV could be used as a viable adjunct to standard methods of intelligence gathering.

After a couple more years testing and refining procedure, the agency was ready to start mining the armed forces for likely candidates in the first ever psychic spying unit under the command of the U.S. government. In the last few months of 1977, project Gondola Wish was culled together with a staff of 11, including future RV stars Joe McMoneagle (designated Viewer #001) and Mel Riley. The more experienced viewers helped to train and monitor viewing sessions for new recruits. This mentoring system remained in place throughout many years and unit name changes. According to McMoneagle, Gondola Wish was basically a recruiting program.

After a few false starts and more testing of potential viewers at SRI, the project was given a new name and semi-permanent quarters at Fort Meade, Maryland. Fort Meade contains NSA headquarters, as well as some offices of the Federal Emergency Management Agency. It is not known whether this proximity is significant or not. At first, the Department of Defense was the only "client" providing projects (called "taskings") to the unit. As word spread, other intelligence agencies also began to take advantage of the new source of HUMINT (HUMan INTelligence.) This is as opposed to SIGINT (SIGnals INTelligence) as in what the NSA looks at. The unit operated under the name "Grill Flame" until late 1983. McMoneagle says that the remote viewers were often the last resort when traditional SIGINT and HUMINT methods came up short. With a 40-60% "hit" average, RV started to look good when everything else had failed.

Due to new techniques developed by Ingo Swann, (who was still training the unit) another name change followed in 1984. Joining the new "Center Lane" group at Ft. Meade was Sergeant Lyn Buchanan. While stationed in Germany and in the company of several officers, Buchanan had crashed an entire NATO computer system through what appeared to be psychokinesis (mind over matter.) One of the dignitaries present was General Albert Stubblebine, who eventually guided the remote viewing program through several stormy years as one if its main supporters among a hostile higher command. After Buchanan's inadvertent display, Stubblebine cornered the flustered Buchanan and told him "Have I got a job for you." Stubblebine also became involved with other aspects of the "New Age" movement, at one point running hot-coal-walking training for officers with self-help guru Tony Robbins.

The Plot Thickens

When Buchanan arrived for duty at the Center Lane unit, one of the first things he was told "unequivocally" was that "We do not do active mental stuff. You will do no active stuff while you're here. Period." Buchanan says that "It was more in the form of a threat." The unit was beginning to come under more scrutiny from the US Legislature, and any controversy (at least any more controversy) would have helped kill the program. Buchanan later added that "One of the guys grinned and said 'well, WE don't do that sort of thing." Buchanan and others were occasionally asked by other agencies to experiment with psychokinetic and possible mind control-type projects. Considering the time frame of all this activity, perhaps one of the projects may have been to destroy or disrupt Libyan or Iraqui computer installations. These experiments are still classified, and to date, no former RV'ers will violate security oaths to talk about them. Yet.

Major David Morehouse, author of the autobiographical *Psychic Warrior* darkly admits to having "gone to some bizarre units and [doing] dastardly things," but will not discuss it further. Other sources say that he and others tied to influence or kill foes like Libyan leader Muamar Quaddafi. Morehouse joined the unit in its next incarnation as project "Sun Streak" which ran from 1985 to 1991. Russell Targ left SRI in 1983, "shocked" over the military applications of remote viewing, and after a few months hiatus, went on a tour of the Soviet Union, exchanging psi research findings with his Russian counterparts. This understandably worried those at SRI and the DIA, and may be the very reason that Targ did it. What he was "shocked" about he never revealed publicly, but it apparently didn't bother former Naval Intelligence /NSA man Puthoff.

Morehouse calls author Jim Schnabel's 1997 book *Remote Viewers: The Secret History of America's Psychic Spies*, a "whitewash" and accuses Schnabel of writing the book under contract for the CIA. Schnabel has countered with a series of postings on the internet basically calling Morehouse a liar (or at least a fabricator.) Morehouse admits to violating his security oath to write his book, but insists that this is the very reason why he can be trusted to give a more accurate picture of the RV program. He is currently a cheerleader for "nonlethal" weapons technology, and sincerely believes that the use of these devices will change the way that future wars are waged—by making them kinder and gentler. He has written a children's cartoon series that feature heroes thwarting the bad guys with nonlethals. He has also completed a screenplay for *Psychic Warrior.* Sylvester Stallone's production company is said to be "very interested."

The Schnabel book contains a few pages on rumors that were trickling out of the Soviet Union at the time, such as experiments where small rabbits and kittens were tortured or killed while hundreds of miles away, the mothers were hooked up to EEGs to see if there was any reaction. In his book Psychic Warfare, Martin Ebon decribes the case of Nina Kulagina who apparently stopped the beating heart of a frog, and induced a rapid heartbeat in a skeptical psychologist. If anything like this occurred in the U.S., Schnabel either wasn't told about it, or didn't write about it. Buchanan and Morehouse suggest otherwise. There is certainly documented proof that research into this area at least held great interest for the US military.

The Unicorn

The enigmatic Ira Einhorn, sometimes euphemistically called "The Unicorn" formed a group of the parapsychological hardcore in the 1970s, dubbing the group the "Psychic Mafia." The objective was to bring the vernacular of parapsychology into the mainstream. Members included Andrija Puahrich, Uri Geller, Jack Sarfatti, and a notable number of other possibles such as EST founder Werner Erhard, Arthur C. Clarke, Fred Alan Wolf, Arthur Koestler, Edgar Mitchell and Jacques Vall_e, all friends and/ or associates. He probably began attracting the wrong sort of attention to himself in the mid-'70s by sending information on mind control devices and theories, parapsychological research, and suppressed science (such as Tesla technolgy) to anyone who requested it (and paid a small fee for the copies and postage.) Writer Walter Bowart documents that Einhorn was for a time an aide to congressman Charlie Rose (D-North Carolina) and demonstrated to him a "helmet" that would subject the user to an incredible VR show. One of the presentations Rose enjoyed (?) was reputedly an alien abduction experience. The inventor of this wonderous device is unknown, but many clues point to Michael Persinger, a Canadian neuroscientist who is more widely known for his thesis that geomagnetic fields are the cause of most UFO experiences. In the late 1950s, another Canadian, Wilder Penfield, proved that religious and hallucinatory experiences could be induced by directly stimulating certain areas of the cerbral cortex with very small amounts of electrical current.

Einhorn was more than willing to share this sort of information, and it is for this reason that some believe he was framed in an intelligence community sting that implicated him for the murder of his girlfriend, found mummified and stuffed in a trunk on Einhorn's porch. He is just about to be extradited from France to serve a sentence on an in absentia verdict that was handed down over 20 years ago. Einhorn and his associates were looking into methods of achieving altered states and enhacing psi through natural methods just before he was arrested.

MJ12 Reborn, or just continued?

With this history in mind, a savvy screenwriter might take four or five index cards and arrange them like this: REMOTE VIEWING/ UFO/ MILITARY-INDUSTRIAL COMPLEX/ MIND CONTROL. He or she wouldn't be too far off the mark. In the years since the CIA decided to reveal its involvement in the field of "psychic spying," other clues have come to light that would bring this flight of fancy out of the realm of dreams and paranoia and into the real world of cutting-edge technology and intelligence operations.

In the past few years, a team of California researchers have discovered that a group of intelligence insiders, leading physicists, and remote viewing veterans may have been gathered under the umbrella of something obstensibly named the "Advanced Theoretical Physics Working Group" to integrate these fields into a cohesive set of new theories about the nature of reality, and ways in which technology can influence the mind, and perhaps more importantly in the near future, how the human mind can influence technology. The group is now apparently defunct and/ or has moved on into its next incarnation, possibly within the organizational matrix of multi-millionaire Robert Bigelow's National Institute for Discovery Science (NIDS.)

The membership roster of this think tank allegedly included such names as Col. John Alexander, Ed Dames, Puthoff, and Col. Philip Corso. One of the civilian members/ consultants may have been famed UFO researcher Jacques Vall_e (him again.) This list is by no means complete. These people and others (like McDonnell Douglas research physicist Dr. Jack Houck) formed the core of something that sounds suspiciously like a latter-day incarnation of the legendary MJ-12. As the alleged members of the original organization were well-versed in fields relevant to the UFO subject at the time (as uncovered by the research of Stanton Friedman) so the ATPWG would be well-suited to grapple with the nature of anomalous aerial phenomena and its attendant science in a modern context. The US military and government has always proved to be about 10-20 years ahead of the public curve in technology R&D. One of the members of the ATPWG has actually remarked that they "plan[ned] and set policy regarding the UFO issue."

Alexander and Dames have admitted to their association with the group, and UFO magazine publisher William Birnes discovered Corso's connection to an earlier incarnation of the ATPWG while researching and writing The *Day After Roswell,* which the two co-authored before Corso's death last year. Alexander disagrees with this partial membership roster, and says that "The ATP work had nothing to do with R.V. or M.C. [mind control]" but will not elaborate. He also says that even this parital membership roster is wrong. Dames, has separately admitted his association.

John Alexander

As many readers may know, Alexander is not only "Discreet Projects Scout" (his listed title) for NIDS, but is also considered the "father of Non-Lethal Weapons." His internet name is "Nonlethal2." Alexander has also just released a book called *Future War,* which brings some of the research in non-lethals into the public eye for the first time. Preliminary reviews called the book "dry" and "boring" and the publishers were apparently worried enough about this to get Tom Clancy to write an introduction—sort of like hiding a dog pill in a ball of cheese. Clancy's name is at the top of the cover and about twice as large as Alexander's. Some observers have called non lethal weapon-ry "the kind of wepaons that don't kill you, but if you're hit by one you'll wish that you WERE dead."

While engaging in person, his allegedly duplicitous nature is known among journalists and researchers, and would reflect his background in military intelligence. After a public speech in 1996, Alexander first denied, then acknowledged his participation with the ATPWG. He also said that the US government was not involved in unwitting mind control experiments against its own population. "We don't do that anymore because its illegal" he said.

Viewer Lyn Buchanan recalls that personnel at Fort Meade had strict orders to turn Alexander away if he tried to enter the unit or talk to the staff. General Stubblebine apparently did not want the remote viewing unit contaminated by anything Alexander would bring, and vice versa. All viewers agree that Alexander never had any-thing to do with the official remote viewing program, although as a special projects officer for the General, Alexander oversaw many alternative intelligence and training programs for the Army's INSCOM (Intelligence and Security Command.)

In October 1980, an article by Col. Alexander appeared in the *Military Review,* a professional journal for leading thinkers and poli-cy makers in the armed forces. "The New Mental Battlefield" described psychotronics research, and the fact that there existed "weapons systems that operate on the power of the mind and whose lethal capacity has already been demonstrated." The mind control realm of psychic warfare was also "well advanced" at the time and "the procedures employed include manipulation of human behavior through use of psychological weapons affecting sight, sound, smell, temperature, electromagnetic energy or sensory deprivation." As examples of the potential for purely mental remote control, Alexander cited early efforts to "heal or cause disease," which could be "trans-mitted over distance, thus inducing illness or death for no apparent cause." Telepathic practice had at that time advanced to the point that a suitably trained individual could "induce hypnotic states up to distances of 1000 kilometers...The use of telepathic hypnosis...holds great potential. This capability could allow agents to be deeply planted, with no conscious knowledge of their programming." Perhaps with a little precognition of his own, Alexander concluded:

"Other mind-to-mind thought induction techniques are also being considered. If perfected, this ability could allow the direct transference of thought via telepathy from one mind, or group of minds, to a selected target audience. The unique factor is that the recipient will not be aware that thoughts have been implanted from an external source. He or she will believe that thoughts are original."

There are a few scenarios for why this information even turned up in a journal that is freely available to anyone with a library card. One is that the *Military Review* may be an attempt to subtly direct R&D policy in the military-industrial world, and the writers and editors are engaing in a sort of lobbying for pet projects. Another is that foreign powers will read the contents and act accordingly. In other words, it may be a deliberate spin control journal designed to give the "enemy" or potential enemies a false sense of current armed forces concerns and developments. Perhaps Col. Alexander may have had all these in mind when he wrote the article. As with many operations engaged in by the intel community, killing many birds with one stone is the most desirable outcome. The trick here is to separate the wheat from the chaff, and there is the rub.

Alexander, Ed Dames, and Morehouse later incorporated PSI-Tech as a consulting firm located in Albuquerque, New Mexico performing remote viewing freelance for private sector clients. After some major disagreements between Morehouse and the others, Morehouse resigned. The only interested member left is Dames, who now runs the company with a small staff as an RV training school from a P.O. box address in Los Angeles (although he may be living in Hawaii at present). Morehouse now bristles whenever Alexander's name is mentioned, but apparently doesn't want to air any dirty laundry in public. Alexander pointed out that he was on the board of directors "at one point" along with General Stubblebine, but did not take an active role apart from occasional consulting duties, adding "PSI-Tech was strictly Dames' company." An incorporation document from the New Mexico State Corporation Commission dated June 24, 1993 lists Alexander as the sole "Director" of PSI-Tech, with Dames as President and Morehouse acting as Vice President.

UFOs Enter the Picture (Don't they always?)

Personnel in the remote viewing project at first inadvertently, and then deliberately, delved into the existence and activities of supposed UFOs and the entities responsible for them. In the course of this research, many viewers discovered that not only could they "see" the craft, but also peer into the mechanisms that kept them aloft. Based on the early experiences of Ingo Swann, this is theoretically possible. Buchanan points out that since there can't be any feedback for this sort of viewing, it is dubious at best. Throughout the years of PSI research, it was discovered that the subjects tended to get better results on subsequent targets if they were told how well they did from time to time. In the realm of UFO remote viewing, the possibility of any sort of feedback is remote. This is where rumor and fact, research and disinformation begin to blend into each other like a watercolor landscape.

The thesis of Colonel Philip Corso's *Day After Roswell* is well known: the debris scattered over a southern New Mexico field on July 3, 1947 was indeed extraterrestrial, and was used to seed technology at the highest levels of private industry over the next few decades. Other sources hint that there is evidence of UFO-type technology developed independent of any saucer crashes. There is evidence on record that anti-gravity research was advanced even at mid-century, when it was referred to as "electrogravitics." A technical paper written in 1956 refers to a successful test of an anti-gravity device at that time. There is less documentation on the development of control systems for these vehicles.

One aspect that Corso emphasized was that the supposed Roswell UFO was controlled by a non-physical interface between the craft and crew. Research scientist Ed May, who was with the SRI program from the early 1980s, and later went on to do more psi research for the Defense Intelligence Agency, worked for Science Applications International Corporation from 1992 to 1994. SAIC is a private corporation located in San Diego where remote viewing and parasychology research was continued after SRI lost their government funding. May issued a memo in 1995 that apparently discussed SAIC programs on possible telepathic remote control of defense systems.

Practical PK

This kind of talent would be useful in the event of the sort of EMF disturbance that would knock out conventional electromagnetic communications, like a nuclear blast. Former Air Force communications officer Dan Sherman's book *Above Black* describes a training program innauguarted in the early 1990s along the same lines as the SAIC research, with similar stated goals. He claims to have been involved in a series of assignments involving telepathic communication through blank computer screens. Sherman also claims to have had a telepathic relationship with a typical "grey" who was involved in the project. The operation had a typically Strangelovian name: "Project Preserve Destiny." Another useful application of telepathic control would be in an advanced, antigravitational aeroform that could perform manuevers with inertial forces that would crush a human pilot's body. If the craft had been successfully designed to withstand internal stresses at high speeds and changes in direction, then it might literally be able to "move at the speed of thought." A craft like this would be virtually invincible to attack by conventional defenses.

The SAIC board of directors has included members such as former NSA director Admiral Bobby Ray Inman, and former CIA Directors John Deutch and Robert Gates. Although it has not been reliably confimed, Dr. Louis Joylon West, famous MKULTRA mind control researcher may have been a board member or consultant for a time as well before his death last year. It's not hard to guess what such a dream team might get up to given the proper budget and encouragement. Too bad notorious CIA psychologist Dr. Ewen Cameron isn't around anymore.

Parasychologist Dr. Dean Radin, author of *The Conscious Universe,* and former research scientist for defense contractor Bell Labs puts it this way:

I'll just say that in general, there's a lot about exotic military hardware— experimental gizmos—most of which is mistaken for UFOs. Some of which can indirectly (not intentionally) cause people to perceive things. You can imagine that having this gigantic electromagnetic thing hovering in the air, it changes the local environment in ways that makes people's brains go funny. That sort of stuff apparently really does go on. It's no coincidence that many of these sightings occur near military bases. It's no coincidence that the military bases also deny it. It's been known since the beginning of Blue Book that sightings cluster around bases more than anywhere else. It raises the likelihood that when you have a climate that has to deny what is going on, combined with exotic hardware and unlimited funding (so you can make really strange devices) that virtually creates UFOs. The unethical part of this is allowing people to sustain what in many cases is an illusion.

It has been nearly twenty years since Col. John Alexander described then-current research into telepathic mind control. In that time, techniques have apparently been perfected to mentally remote control complex machines. The commercial division of the Princeton Engineering Anomalies Research group last year announced their plans to release a "psychic switch" onto the consumer market. This chrome-covered box is like a psychokinetic "clapper," allowing the user to turn appliances off and on through the simple power of intention. Since cutting-edge military hardware is generally 10-20 years ahead of the private sector, we can be nearly certain that rockets are being launched by sheer willpower as you read this.

The interface between mind and matter may be nearing a zero-point. The study of the etheric interaction between minds, or the unilateral effects of one upon another were in their infancy 20 years ago. At the turn of a new century, the words of the Firesign Theatre have acquired renewed meaning: "Your brain may no longer be the boss." It might be somebody else's.

Greg Bishop is editor and publisher of *The Excluded Middle* magazine. Yes, it's actually printed on paper that people can hold and carry around. *The Excluded Middle* started out as a UFO zine, with equal parts humor and spirituality, new science, psychedelics, and stories about flying saucer contactees from the 1950s. Recently, some of that "conspiracy" stuff has started to creep in for some reason. He has also hosted a music and talk show on pirate FM station KBLT in Los Angeles called *The Hungry Ghost*. His writing has appeared in *UFO Magazine*, *Magical Blend*, *GNOSIS*, *The Nose*, *Book Happy*, *Crash Collusion*, in the anthologies *KOOKS*, and *Zen In The Art of Close Encounters*, and authorized and otherwise at various places on the internet. He lives in Los Angeles but can be found on the road in the Great American Desert when he's not at home. exclmid@primenet.com
www.primenet.com/~exclmid
P.O. Box 481077 Los Angeles, CA 90048

Special thanks to:
John Alexander, Lyn Buchanan, Joe McMoneagle, David Morehouse, Dr. Dean Radin, and Richard Sarradet. To Bill Moore for starting the Sisyphean ball rolling, and to other sources who shall remain nameless. Robin Ramsay of *Lobster* magazine. The Texufornia Illuminaughty. And Kenn Thomas, of course.

Sources:

Interviews:
Joe McMoneagle — December 16, 1998.
David Morehouse — February 24, 1999.
Lyn Buchanan — June 10, 1999.
Dean Radin — November 18, 1997.

e-mail:
John Alexander — June 13-14, 1999.

Lectures/Presentations:
Psi + mc2 + R&D = MJ12
Lecture by Melinda Leslie on August 3, 1998 at the International UFO congress, Laughlin NV.
Research conducted by Leslie and Randy Koppang.

Books:

Constantine, Alex *Psychic Dictatorship In The USA*. Portland, OR: Feral House, 1995.
Corso, Philip, and William J. Birnes, *The Day After Roswell*. New York: Pocket Books, 1997.
Ebon, Martin, *Psychic Warfare: Threat or Illusion?* New York: McGraw

Hill, 1983.

Jahn, Robert G. and Brenda J. Dunne, *Margins of Reality.* San Diego, CA: Harcourt, Brace and Co. 1987.

Keith, Jim, *Mind Control, World Control.* Kempton, IL: Adventures Unlimited Press, 1997.

McMoneagle, Joseph, *Mind Trek: Exploring Consciousness, Time, and Space Through Remote Viewing.* Charlottesville, VA: Hampton Roads Publishing, 1993.

Morehouse, David, *Psychic Warrior.* New York: St. Martin's Press, 1996.

ibid, *Nonlethal Weapons: War Without Death.* Westport, CN: Praeger Publishers, 1996.

Puthoff, Harold, and Russell Targ, *Mind-Reach: Scientists Look at Psychic Ability.* New York: Dell Publishing Co. 1978.

Radin, Dean, *The Conscious Universe.* San Francisco: Harper Collins Publishers, 1997.

Schnabel, Jim, *Remote Viewers: The Secret History of America's Psychic Spies.* New York: Dell Publishing, 1997.

Sinclair, Upton, *Mental Radio.* Springfield Il, Charles C. Thomas Publisher, 1930.

Targ, Russell and Keith Harary, *The Mind Race.* New York, Villiard Books, 1983.

Vallee, Jacques, *Messengers of Deception.* Berkeley, And/Or Press, 1979.

Articles:

Kress, Kenneth, "Parapsychology In Intelligence: A Personal Review and Conclusions" *Journal of Scientific Exploration,* Vol. 13, No. 1. 1999.

Miley, Michael, "Remote Viewing and Alien Targets: Room With an (Alien) View" *UFO Magazine,* Vol. 11, No. 3. 1996.

ibid, "Room With an Alien View: Part Two," *UFO Magazine,* Vol. 13, No. 5. 1998.

Targ, Russell, "Comments On Parapsychology In Intelligence: A Personal Review and Conclusions," *Journal of Scientific Exploration,* Vol. 13, No. 1. 1999.

Ibid and Harold Puthoff, "Information Transmission Under Conditions of Sensory Shielding" *Nature,* Vol 252, No. 5476. 1974.

Sterling, Robert, "John Alexander-Remote Viewer or Remote Controller?" From the *Konformist* website: http://www.konformist.com/

Victorian, Armen, "Remote Viewing and the U.S. Intelligence Community," *Lobster,* Issue #31. 1997.

Internet:

The BB (Brother Blue-now defunct): http://www.brotherblue.org/index.html

Doc Hambone: http://www.io.com/~hambone/index.html

The Konformist: http://www.konformist.com/

Lobster: http://www.knowledge.co.uk/lobster

National Institute For Discovery Science: http://www.accessnv.com/nids

Steamshovel Press: http://www.umsl.edu/~skthoma/

Superpowers of the Human Biomind (Ingo Swann): http://www.biomindsuperpowers.com

THE CHRIST CONSPIRACY • ACHARYA S

"Exposes the conspiracy of the soul..."
- Kenn Thomas, *Steamshovel Press!*

Available from Adventures Unlimited (815) 253-6390, The Book Tree (800) 700-TREE, or order it from your favorite bookseller.

In this highly controversial and explosive book archaeologist, historian, mythologist and linguist Acharya S marshals an enormous amount of startling evidence to demonstrate that Christianity and the story of Jesus Christ were created by members of various secret societies, mystery schools and religions in order to unify the Roman Empire under one state religion. In making In making such a fabrication, this multinational multinational cabal drew upon a multitude of myths and rituals that already existed long before the Christian era, and reworked them for centuries into the story and religion passed down today.

Contrary to popular belief, no single man exists at the genesis of Christianity but many characters rolled into one do. The majority of these characters personified the ubiquitous solar myth. Their adventures were well known as reflected by such popular deities as Mithra, Heracles /Hercules, Dionysus, and many others throughout the Roman Empire and beyond. The story of Jesus as portrayed in the Gospels is nearly identical in detail to that of the earlier savior-gods Krishna and Horus. These redeemer tales are similar not because they reflect the actual exploits of a variety of men who did and said identical things, but because they represent the same extremely ancient body of knowledge that revolved around the celestial bodies and natural forces. The result of this mythmaking became "The Christ Conspiracy." ISBN 0-932813-74-7 • 256 pps • 6x9 • $14.95.

AVAILABLE FROM STEAMSHOVEL PRESS

The Search for the Saucers Begins!
Flying Saucers of Los Angeles, Introduction by Kenn Thomas, Manuscript by DeWayne Johnson, Commentary by David Hatcher Childress.

Beginning with a previously unpublished manuscript by DeWayne B. Johnson entitled *Flying Saucers:: Fact or Fiction?*. *Flying Saucers Over Los Angeles,* chronicles who saw what, where and when during the earliest years of the flying saucer flap beginning June 24, 1947. It adds new information to such renown cases as the Roswell crash and the Maury Island incident and it continues to lesser-known sightings. *Flying Saucers Over Los Angeles* presents a contemporaneous view of the earliest UFO excitement in 1950s America, unvarnished by the accumulated speculation of the last 46 years. A more detailed account of the many early sightings has never before been published! The book also presents one of the first analyses of the sociological and psychological dimensions of the UFO experience, written from a vantage point of certainty that flying saucers are real–borne out by the actual news and witness accounts.

With a 16-page color insert of rare UFO photos and early flying saucer artwork, *Flying Saucers Over Los Angeles* recreates the original excitement of the hysteria that swept across America Copies of the original news articles are provided in an appendix, with additional news clippings from *The New York Times* and other papers. Add to your knowledge of the parapolitical history of UFOs and relive the time when people first started watching the sky for the mysterious saucers! $18 postpaid

***Steamshovel Press*, PO Box 23715, St. Louis, MO 63121, www.umsl.edu/~skthoma**

AVAILABLE FROM STEAMSHOVEL PRESS

The Octopus: Secret Government and the Death of Danny Casolaro by Kenn Thomas and Jim Keith, Feral House

Picks up where Casolaro left off. Danny Casolaro's surviving handwritten notes and drafts of his manuscript provide part of the basis for this book, which also relies on interviews with key players in the tale, affidavits, court records, congressional documents, and mainstream and non-mainstream sources to present a more comprehensive view of Casolaro's Octopus than has been available previously. The Octopus was Casolaro's name for an intelligence cabal whose involvement in a list of notorious contemporary political crimes he had documented in his unfinished book. His toe-hold was PROMIS, a super-surveillance software misappropriated from a company called Inslaw by Ed Meese's Justice Department and sold illegally to police agencies around the world. PROMIS had been modified, according to Casolaro's chief inform-ant, a shadowy denizen of the intelligence underworld named Michael Riconosciuto, to include a "back door," allowing the US to spy on its illegal clients. Riconosciuto also helped develop Contra War chemical and biowarfare weapons on the tribal lands of the Cabazon Indians of Indio, California, weapons possibly used in the 1983 Beirut blast that left over 300 American and French military personnel dead. Casolaro's research also looked at bizarre murders among the Cabazon Indians involving administrators of the tribal land; the privatization of CIA dirty tricks through the notorious Wackenhut security firm, the policemen for both the Cabazons and the mysterious Area 51, home of secret spy planes and rumored UFOs; Vietnam MIAs; manufacturing corruption at Hughes Aircraft; the human genome project; even the Illuminati secret societies of the 18th century. 185 pages, 6x9, photographs, hardbound, $23.00 postpaid.

Steamshovel Press, **PO Box 23715, St. Louis, MO 63121 www.umsl.edu/~skthoma**

Popular Alienation: A Steamshovel Reader edited by Kenn Thomas

The Back Issue Anthology: Abbie Hoffman's death seen as an assassination; the role of George Bush in the death of JFK; Black Holes and the Trilateral commission; Esoteric conspiratorialism; Kalifornia prisons; Presidency-As-Theatre; the American Nazis; deconstruction of Noam Chomsky; tabloid disinformation; JFK's LSD mistress, Mary Pinchot Meyer; Shroud of Turin conspiracies; the prison files of Wilhelm Reich; Danny Casolaro, Inslaw and the Octopus; the Ustica plane disaster; Tim Leary's Party; the Mothman; Roswell; Holocaust Revisionism; the Gemstone File; the Secret Service files of Mae Brussels; Area 51, the Aurora and the Moonbase; Bill Clinton's conspiratorial mentor, Carroll Quigley; the madness of Ezra Pound; anti-gravity research of secret society Nazis; cattle mutilation file of the FBI; vampire deities and much more!

BONUS! Includes never before published Steamshovel/ Press #13, a virtual issue contained only in this volume, including Carl Sagan's 1962 affirmation of life in space; new information on the Gemstone thesis; an Oklahoma City bombing rant; update on mystery oil man and yeti sleuth Tom Slick; return of the Men In Black; Willis Carto on varieties of fascist experience; Carlos Castaneda conspiracies; undoing the Vietnam of Robert McNamara. 360 pages, 8.5x11, quality soft cover, $23, post paid.

Steamshovel Press, **PO Box 23715, St. Louis, MO 63121 www.umsl.edu/~skthoma**

AVAILABLE FROM STEAMSHOVEL PRESS

130

TRIUMPH OF THE HUMAN SPIRIT: The Greatest Achievements of the Human Soul and How Its Power Can Change Your Life by **Paul Tice.** A triumph of the human spirit happens when we know we are right about something, put our heart into achieving its goal, and then succeed. There is no better feeling. People throughout history have triumphed while fighting for the highest ideal of all – spiritual truth. Some of these people and movements failed, other times they changed the course of history. Those who failed only did so on a physical level, when they were eliminated through violence. Their spirit lives on. This book not only documents the history of spiritual giants, it shows you how you can achieve your own spiritual triumph. Various exercises will strengthen your soul and reveal its hidden power. In today's world we are free to explore the truth without fear of being tortured or executed. As a result, the rewards are great. You will discover your true spiritual power with this work and will be able to tap into it. This is the perfect book for all those who believe in spiritual freedom and have a passion for the truth. **(1999) • 295 pages • 6 x 9 • trade paperback • $19.95 • ISBN 1-885395-57-4**

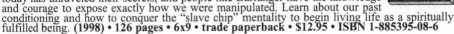

PAST SHOCK: The Origin of Religion and Its Impact on the Human Soul by **Jack Barranger. Introduction by Paul Tice.** Twenty years ago, Alvin Toffler coined the term "future shock" – a syndrome in which people are overwhelmed by the future. *Past Shock* suggests that events which happened thousands of years ago very strongly impact humanity today. This book reveals incredible observations on our inherited "slave chip" programming and how w've been conditioned to remain spiritually ignorant. Barranger exposes what he calls the "pretender gods," advanced beings who were not divine, but had advanced knowledge of scientific principles which included genetic engineering. Our advanced science of today has unraveled their secrets, and people like Barranger have the knowledge and courage to expose exactly how we were manipulated. Learn about our past conditioning and how to conquer the "slave chip" mentality to begin living life as a spiritually fulfilled being. **(1998) • 126 pages • 6x9 • trade paperback • $12.95 • ISBN 1-885395-08-6**

GOD GAMES: What Do You Do Forever? by **Neil Freer. Introduction by Zecharia Sitchin.** This new book by the author of Breaking the Godspell clearly outlines the entire human evolutionary scenario. While Sitchin has delineated what happened to humankind in the remote past based on ancient texts, Freer outlines the implications for the future. We are all creating the next step we need to take as we evolve from a genetically engineered species into something far beyond what we could ever imagine. We can now play our own "god games." We are convinced that great thinkers in the future will look back on this book, in particular, as being the one which opened the door to a new paradigm now developing. Neil Freer is a brilliant philosopher who recognizes the complete picture today, and is far ahead of all others who wonder what really makes us tick, and where it is that we are going. This book will make readers think in new and different ways. **(1998) • 310 pages • 6 x 9 • trade paperback • $19.95 • ISBN 1-885395-39-6**

OF HEAVEN AND EARTH: Essays Presented at the First Sitchin Studies Day. Edited by **Zecharia Sitchin.** Zecharia Sitchin's previous books have sold millions around the world. This book contains further information on his incredible theories about the origins of mankind and the intervention by intelligences beyond the Earth. This book offers the complete proceedings of the first Sitchin Studies Day. Sitchin's keynote address opens the book, followed by six other prominent speakers whose work has been influenced by Sitchin. The other contributors include two university professors, a clergyman, a UFO expert, a philosopher, and a novelist – who joined Zecharia Sitchin to describe how his findings and conclusions have affected what they teach and preach. They all seem to agree that the myths of ancient peoples were actual events as opposed to being figments of imaginations. Another point of agreement is in Sitchin's work being the early part of a new paradigm – one that is already beginning to shake the very foundations of religion, archaeology and our society in general. **(1996) • 164 pages • 5 1/2 x 8 1/2 • trade paperback • $14.95 • ISBN 1-885395-17-5**

FLYING SERPENTS AND DRAGONS: The Story of Mankind's Reptilian Past, By **R.A. Boulay.** Revised and expanded edition. This highly original work deals a shattering blow to all our preconceived notions about our past and human origins. Worldwide legends refer to giant flying lizards and dragons which came to this planet and founded the ancient civilizations of Mesopotamia, Egypt, India and China. Who were these reptilian creatures? This book provides the answers to many of the riddles of history such as what was the real reason for man's creation, why did Adam lose his chance at immortality in the Garden of Eden, who were the Nefilim who descended from heaven and mated with human women, why the serpent take such a bum rap in history, why didn't Adam and Eve wear clothes in Eden, what were the "crystals" or "stones" that the ancient gods fought over, why did the ancient Sumerians call their major gods USHUMGAL, which means literally "great fiery, flying serpent," what was the role of the gigantic stone platform at Baalbek, and what were the "boats of heaven" in ancient Egypt and the "sky chariots" of the Bible? **(1997, 1999) • 276 pages • 6 x 9 • trade paperback • $19.95 • ISBN 1-885395-38-8**

Call for our FREE BOOK TREE CATALOG with over 1000 titles. Order from your favorite bookseller, or we accept Visa, MC, AmEx, or send check or money order (in USD) for the total amount plus 4.50 shipping for 1-3 books (and .50¢ thereafter). The Book Tree • PO Box 724 • Escondido, CA 92033 • (760) 489-5079 • Visit www.thebooktree.com • **Call today (800) 700-TREE**

Steamshovel Press Returns!

ISSUE #16 1998

$6.00

666

MIND KONTROL
PARANOID IKONOGRAPHY
MANUFACTURING CONSUMPTION
SAUCER STELLON
CUBES, CURLS, AND CORRESPONDENCE
MUCH MORE!

The FINDERS

Counter-Culture OR Counter-Intelligence? An Interview with Marion Pettie

Printed in the USA
CPSIA information can be obtained
at www.ICGtesting.com
CBHW030057160524
8657CB00008B/186